BIKE
WITH A VIEW

Easy / moderate mountain bike rides to scenic destinations

COLORADO'S FRONT RANGE AND CENTRAL MOUNTAINS

**WRITTEN AND PHOTOGRAPHED BY
MARK DOWLING**

CONCEPTS IN WRITING

Denver, Colorado

Cover Photo by Mark Dowling: A tunnel of aspen leaves over the Boreas Pass Road above Breckenridge, Colorado. Note: The bicycle rider in the photo, Saundra Dowling, removed her helmet for this photo session only. Please always wear a helmet.

BIKE WITH A VIEW

Easy / moderate mountain bike rides to scenic destinations
COLORADO'S FRONT RANGE AND CENTRAL MOUNTAINS

WRITTEN AND PHOTOGRAPHED BY MARK DOWLING

Published by: **CONCEPTS IN WRITING**

1135 S. Garfield St.
Denver, Colorado 80210

All photography by Mark Dowling
All maps, book and cover design by Saundra Dowling

Mountain biking is an activity with inherent risks. All participants should be aware of these risks and be willing to take personal responsibility for their actions while riding. The author, Concepts in Writing, its staff and management recommend mountain biking participants seek professional instruction on the areas of mountain biking that they are not knowledgeable in, including the risks associated with these areas.

Library of Congress Card Number: 93-91041

ISBN 0-9639697-0-6 $12.95 Softcover
Printed in the United States of America

TABLE OF CONTENTS

Ride Directory

Ride Directory, continued

RIDE	PAGE	ABILITY LEVEL	NEAREST TOWN
Biking Oases	P. 53		
Blue Lakes	P. 55	Easy II	Breckenridge
Dillon Reservoir	P. 59	Easy I	Frisco
Dowdy Lake	P. 63	Easy I	Fort Collins
O'Haver Lake	P. 67	Easy I	Poncha Springs/Salida
Rampart Reservoir	P. 71	Moderate I	Woodland Park
Turquoise Lake	P. 75	Moderate II	Leadville
Vasquez Creek	P. 79	Easy I	Winter Park
Waterton Canyon	P. 83	Easy I	Denver
Bike into History	P. 87		
Boreas Pass	P. 93	Easy II	Breckenridge
Midland Bike Trail	P. 97	Moderate II	Buena Vista
New Santa Fe Trail	P. 101	Easy I	Palmer Lake
St. Elmo	P. 105	Easy II	Buena Vista
Waldorf Mine	P. 109	Moderate I	Georgetown

ABILITY LEVELS

EASY I: Mostly level, little climbing, no rocks, fairly short-under 10 miles in most cases.

EASY II: A few short climbs, a few rocks or obstacles, fairly short-under 10 miles in most cases.

MODERATE I: Some longer climbs at higher elevations, moderately rocky terrain, moderate length-8 to 12 miles.

MODERATE II: Extended climbing possible, a few very rocky "techincal riding" sections, moderate length-10 to 16 miles.

Acknowledgments

Writing and self-publishing a book is an enormous undertaking, but it would not be possible without the help of several individuals and agencies.

My wife, Saundra Dowling, contributed many hours to this project. She created all the beautiful maps in this book and designed the entire book, including the cover. She went on several rides with me and even posed for the cover photo! J. Barry Winter's professional photography guidance was invaluable, as was Bert Matthews' advice on ride choices and mountain biking in general. All the government agencies, including the U.S. Forest Service, Bureau of Reclamation and the numerous small communities I visited, helped a great deal with my research.

An *easy* mountain bike ride?

Several years ago, after having ridden a touring bike for 15 years and thousands of miles, I decided to plunge into mountain biking.

Unfortunately, *plunge* is the key word here. On my first attempt, I pushed the bike up half the ride and gritted my teeth as I scraped and skidded down the other half. On my second try, I rode with an "experienced" mountain biker who took me on a trail only a little less terrifying. (At one moment, his entire body disappeared into "a little rut" in the dirt road.) And I could not tell you what any of the scenery on these trails looked like — I was too preoccupied with life preservation to notice.

This scenario is repeated countless times by many would-be mountain bikers. They buy or rent a mountain bike and think, "I'm going to ride on a *real* mountain trail." Their glee is soon dampened by a treacherous ride that is much too difficult for them. Some of these riders end up giving up the sport before they ever begin. One experienced road rider I know told me, "That new mountain bike is collecting quite a bit of dust in my basement."

Mountain bikes were developed in the 1970s with the original intent of getting exercise in a natural, car-free environment, but also as a way to travel to some naturally beautiful places that would take all day or even several days to hike to. Unfortunately, for some riders, the physical challenge has overshadowed the visual gain that can be attained. What many riders *see* often takes a back seat to how fast they get there and how difficult it is to get there.

In this book, I have tried to give readers and riders the best of both worlds: Rides that have some interesting "visual destinations," but don't require the athletic prowess of a triathlete. On all the rides, you will be able to get a decent amount of exercise, but they are not so difficult that you are concentrating more on staying on the trail than viewing the scenery around you. By choosing the right rides, you, too, will enjoy a bike with a view.

A few mountain biking tips

I don't intend to launch into a full-fledged instructional thesis on mountain biking; there are gazillions of other books out there that do that. I will, however, give you a few basic mountain biking tips to get you on your way.

LOCATION, LOCATION, LOCATION

Any real estate agent will tell you that there are three things to look for when buying property: "Location, location, location." This tongue-in-cheek cliché does have some validity to it. You can always improve or change the house itself, but rarely the location.

The same holds true for mountain biking. You could buy the latest, most expensive bike available, but you still won't enjoy yourself if you're in the wrong location or on the wrong trail. Picking the right place to bike is the most important aspect of mountain biking; choosing the right equipment is second.

When you're first starting out in mountain biking, it's important to choose a trail that's very easy — maybe just a little more difficult than riding on pavement. It's also important that the trail goes someplace interesting. I don't know what's worse: Getting terrified to death or bored to death on your first ride!

PROGRESSIVE RIDE PLAN

As you gain more confidence, you should graduate to more and more challenging rides, but make sure to get plenty of practice *at each level.* I can't emphasize this point enough. You can't expect to ride an "Easy I" trail on Monday and a "Moderate II" trail on Friday.

Using the rides in this book, I have suggested some rides for beginning and moderate riders to do at each level. I refer to the ability ratings I have created as Easy I and II and Moderate I and II. Read the explanation of these levels, which appears right after the table of contents and in the "using this guide" sections of this book.

Beginners

Beginners with little or no off-road experience should ride on relatively flat, rock-free *unpaved* trails, such as dirt roads. The problem here is, many dirt roads have some fairly steady motor vehicle traffic. In the Denver area, an excellent easy dirt trail is the Highline Canal, which weaves through the south Denver suburbs. In this book, I recommend these rides for beginners: **Waterton Canyon, New Santa Fe Trail, O'Haver Lake, Dowdy Lake, Vasquez Creek and Dillon Reservoir.** I have classified this level of rider as **Easy I.**

Advanced beginners

These riders have ridden several times on the easy trails and are ready for something a little more challenging, with a little more climbing, curves, and a few rocks and obstacles in the trail. I recommend these rides: **Chair Rocks, Blue Lakes, Flume Trail, Boreas Pass, Waldorf Mine, Elk Meadow, Alderfer/Three Sisters (loop 2) and Switzerland Trail.** I have classified these riders as **Easy II.**

Moderate riders

These riders want a little more challenge still, but don't want to kill themselves. These trails have more length, climbing and more rocky sections. I recommend these rides: **Rampart Reservoir, Turquoise Lake, St. Elmo, Kenosha Pass** and **Alderfer/ Three Sisters (loop 1).** I have classified these riders as **Moderate I, Moderate II.**

CHOOSING EQUIPMENT

Again, I won't launch into a long lecture on biking equipment, but there are at least a couple of things you should know.

The number one factor that should be considered when either buying or renting a bike is size. Sizing is a little complicated, but it can be boiled down to this: When standing flat-footed over the mountain bike with biking shoes or sneakers on, there should be about three inches of clearance between the bike's top tube and the rider's crotch. This is to allow leeway for falling and negotiating obstacles on the trail. On a touring bike, the clearance is only about an inch or so. The best way to size a mountain bike is to go (during an off-peak time) into a bike shop that knows how to size a bike. After getting your size, write it down and walk out of the shop. Now try several bikes of this size, either by renting or borrowing friends' bikes. Now you'll know what you'll be comfortable with.

SHOCK VALUE

Another big decision in the bike-buying process is whether or not to buy shocks. Mountain bike shocks have become very popular in the last few years. They *do* smooth out the bumps in a ride quite a bit. However, many bikers — even experienced riders on their second or third bikes — are beginning to re-think shocks. Because they do make a ride much smoother, you have a tendency to go much faster than you would without shocks. In some cases, more speed can mean a better chance of "catching" something like a rock or log, flinging you onto or off of the trail. If you think you'll be able to control your speed, you probably won't have this problem.

WHAT TO BRING WITH YOU

Deciding what equipment to bring with you on the trail is directly related to where you ride. This is because you're riding in Colorado, where the elevations are high and the weather is very changeable. Every ride in this book is over 5,000 feet above sea level, and some are between 7,000 and 10,500 feet. In the Rockies, gaining 1,000 feet in elevation is like traveling 500 miles north. The air is cooler, the snow either gets deeper or the chance of snow (yes, even in the summer!) gets greater. In the summer, severe thunderstorms are very common in the mountains.

For this reason, I suggest the following equipment:

Bare essentials:

- Bike helmet
- Tire pump
- 2 full water bottles
- Small first aid kit
- Nonperishable food
- Rain suit
- Tire irons
- Adjustable wrench
- Map
- 1 Phillips, 1 regular screwdriver
- Bike gloves
- Patch kit or tube
- Allen wrench kit

"Extras" that are nice to have:

- Chain-break tool
- Rubber or surgical gloves
- Plastic bags big enough to put feet into
- Lightweight emergency space blanket
- 3-way "Y" socket wrench that fits all bike's bolts
- Lightweight full-fingered gloves
- Some fresh food

In the "bare essentials" category, always make sure you have enough water and a pump and patch kit. At the beginning of the season, I always put the bare essentials into my seat pack and keep them there, including the emergency food, such as an energy, candy or granola bar. Before you empty your father's tool box into a bike bag, check out the new, high-tech "combi" bike tools that ingeniously combine many tools into one small package.

On each ride, I bring fresh food. While even beginning riders remember to bring water, many forget food. Remember, mountain biking requires much more energy per mile than road biking. If you are having trouble with a ride, an empty stomach and the "hunger shakes" will only add to your anxiety. On the other hand, a mini-picnic or a full-fledged feast is a great way to enhance the beautiful places you'll be riding to.

In the "nice to have" category, don't laugh at my rubber gloves and plastic bags! Both of these are extremely compact and lightweight (and inexpensive) life-savers in a rain storm. Put the bags over your socks inside your shoes, *before* your feet get soaked! In the fall and spring, you will use the full-fingered fabric gloves quite a bit.

You don't need a suitcase to hold all of this. I fit most of these things in an expandable seat back. I put the rain suit on my back rack. Enlarged fanny packs are also becoming very popular. Try not to use a heavy backpack; your back will tell you why after 10 miles or so. I found the back rack to be a good investment because I also use my mountain bike to run errands in the city.

Don't fall for the argument: "But it adds so much weight to your bike." If you're reading this book, you're probably not worrying about catching the next guy in a mountain bike race. When you need these things, you won't regret taking them along.

FINDING YOUR WAY THERE — AND BACK
Most of the rides in this book are relatively short and a few even skirt some developed areas. Still, it is always possible to get lost if you don't take the proper precautions.

You should know as much as possible about the area before you leave your house. Read the ride description in this book, study the accompanying map and purchase the recommended maps and carry a map with you if you're unfamiliar with the area.

Colorado's weather is extremely unpredictable, but you can control it — by not going out in it! Here is a typical biking outing. A group drives an hour or so to the biking area they have planned to go to all week. When they get there, the clouds look extremely "heavy" and there is a stiff breeze blowing. One or two of the party's members suggest that maybe they shouldn't go. These cries in the wilderness are quickly squelched by peer pressure and they leave on the ride. Three miles later, they are caught in a vicious rainstorm that also packs a wicked surprise: hail! (The space blanket would be extremely useful here.)

Another common mistake is leaving on a ride near or at sunset because it's "romantic." This is fine for a quick 3 or 4-mile trail that you've ridden on many times before and is well populated with hikers and bikers. But in most cases, give yourself several hours of daylight to do the ride.

RIDING TECHNIQUES
Riding a mountain bike is just like riding a "normal" (road) bike, right? If I have ridden a road bike, I'll have no problem with a mountain bike, right? Well, not quite. The rider must concentrate on a few fundamental technique changes to tackle the dirt road or trail to have a safe, comfortable and fun ride.

The number one change is to *not* stand up on the pedals and get off the saddle while climbing. This is fine on pavement, but on dirt, it saps the valuable traction from the rear wheel and the rider ends up "spinning." The bike stops, and on steeper hills, the rider may end up off the bike. To correct this, try to keep your weight over the rear wheel as much as possible, even if it means stretching out your body a little.

"Scaling" logs, rocks and other obstacles is another important skill for the new rider. The trick here is to start small and keep your weight on the rear of the bike. Start with small twigs, tree limbs or mounds of dirt. As you approach them, lighten your front wheel by putting more weight toward the rear of the bike and simultaneously pulling slightly (not jerking) up on the handlebars. Gradually graduate to larger objects, such as small logs on *flat terrain.* Then do it on increasingly steeper grades.

Going downhill frightens some new riders more than anything else. Again, start small and take it easy. Try to relax and look ahead on the trail as far as possible to plan your course. Try not to brake constantly; this will only make you skid more and may cause you to fall.

RESPECTING THE ENVIRONMENT
If you do five simple things, you'll do a lot for the environment:

1. Always stay on the trail — no exceptions.
2. Try not to make any new ruts, even if it means carrying your bike around the wet spots.
3. Go over, not around, those "water breaks" in the trail. They're those long rubber or wooden things that go across the entire width of trail. They serve an important purpose. In a storm, they divert rushing streams of water off the trail. If you make paths around them, the trail becomes the stream bed.
4. Take out all trash, including banana peels. Please keep the trail as beautiful as you found it.
5. Keep your bike out of all designated wilderness areas; these are for hikers only.

Using this guide

The following ride descriptions and maps were done to give the rider a good idea of what she'll find on the ride, but there is plenty of room for exploration. Both the maps and descriptions should give you a general idea of the highlights of each trail; they are by no means a mile-by-mile manual for the ride. You are encouraged to get the maps suggested for each ride.

Following are explanations of the preliminary ride information at the beginning of each ride description.

DISTANCE: The mileage for each ride was calculated from the parking area recommended by using a bicycle computer. The exact mileage may not exactly match the reading on your computer, but it should be very close. For riders without computers, I have tried to provide physical descriptions of particular points in the trail along with the mileage readings.

ABILITY LEVELS: Every ride is classified by one of four levels:

Easy I: Mostly level, little climbing, no rocks, fairly short — under 10 miles in most cases.

Easy II: A few short climbs, a few rocks or obstacles, fairly short — under 10 miles in most cases.

Moderate I: Some longer climbs at higher elevations, moderately rocky terrain, moderate length — 8-12 miles.

Moderate II: Extended climbing possible, a few very rocky "technical riding" sections, moderate length — 10-16 miles.

TRAIL TYPE: All rides are classified as singletrack, doubletrack or dirt road.

Singletrack usually refers to a combination hiking/biking trail with a "single track." No motor vehicles are allowed on these trails, but horses and dogs may be; take the appropriate precautions.

Doubletrack usually refers to a trail that was once used as a motor vehicle road, but motor vehicles are now prohibited. The term "abandoned dirt road" is also used for this type of trail.

Dirt road is a road used by 4-wheel drive and/or 2-wheel drive vehicles, in most cases. The term "maintained dirt road" is also used for this type of trail.

CLIMBS: I have tried to point out the major climbs or hills that may concern beginning and moderate riders. By no means did I describe every little hill on the ride. On the rides where the entire first half is a climb to a certain mountain pass or the Continental Divide, the term "continuous climb" is used.

ELEVATION RANGE: This is the range of the approximate altitude in a particular ride. The figures given are lowest and highest elevations for that particular ride.

MAPS: The appropriate maps for each ride are listed. Four types are referred to:

United States Forest Service (USFS): These maps are published by the Forest Service and one map covers either one or two of the several National Forests that blanket Colorado. These are good maps for general orientation and they are a much larger scale than a Colorado state map. However, they are not topographic maps and some of them are outdated.

United States Geological Survey (USGS): These topographic maps are used by "dyed-in-the-wool" hikers and other outdoors people because of their detail. They show elevations, hiking trails and roads. They are extremely large scale; you usually have to buy one map per hike or ride.

Trails Illustrated: These waterproof, tear proof topographic maps combine several USGS maps in one map and they also indicate elevations, hiking trails, mountain bike routes and cross-country ski trails.

Colorado Trail maps: This is a fine set of large-scale topographic maps that cover the entire Colorado Trail from Denver to Durango. Proceeds help support the Colorado Trail Foundation, which maintains the trail. The maps are available at Colorado REI stores, or you can write to the foundation: Colorado Trail Foundation, 548 Pineson Trail, Golden, CO 80401.

The Forest Service maps are available at the Rocky Mountain Regional Office of the Forest Service in Golden (see the back of the book). The Forest Service, Trails Illustrated and USGS maps are available at REI and North Face stores in the Denver area or at most good outdoor stores in other states. For map heaven, go to Maps Unlimited, 899 Broadway, Denver (303-623-4299).

DRIVING TIME FROM DENVER: The driving time was calculated from I-25 and Colorado Boulevard in Denver. Adjust the time appropriately from where you start.

VISTAS AND VALLEYS

When Stephen Long (Long's Peak) and Zebulon Pike (Pike's Peak) explored Colorado in the early part of the 19th century, they were awestruck by what they discovered: mountain peaks that seemed to reach the heavens, wild rivers and countless new plant species.

The small bands of explorers often took months to reach the Rockies. The expeditions usually consisted of an odd assortment of explorers, naturalists and artists who would document what they saw to show proof to expedition sponsors.

Today, we can drive through what it took explorers days or weeks to traverse. And if that's not quick enough, we fly over everything in an hour or so.

But despite the developers, planners and map-makers who have charted every square mile of Colorado, much of the state remarkably resembles what the first explorers saw. Thanks to the existence of large tracts of publicly owned land, you could hike for days without seeing a condo, housing development or other signs of "civilization." In some of Colorado's mountain counties, more than 80 percent of the land is publicly owned!

Colorado has 54 peaks 14,000 feet or more above sea level ("fourteeners") and more than 800 peaks above 11,000 feet.

While the rides in this book don't climb any of the fourteeners, you will get a fairly close-up view of them, including Pike's Peak (Chair Rocks and Rampart Reservoir rides), and Grays and Torreys Peaks (Waldorf Mine ride).

You will also experience incredible geographic diversity. For example, the rides at Matthews/Winters Park and Green Mountain resemble the terrain in southwestern Colorado: deep red rocks, dry terrain and sweeping views of the valley and foothills. Just a 20-minute drive from these trails, the Elk Meadow trail in Evergreen is an alpine retreat with mountain meadows and thick groves of aspen and pine.

While we won't be the first to discover any "new territory," we can still have a sense of adventure and accomplishment by journeying to these beautiful places on our own power.

ALDERFER/ THREE SISTERS PARK
A lonely pine tree is wedged in the rocks on the Brothers Lookout, a great vantage point to see the entire Evergreen area. While the climb to the Lookout is a tough one, the view is worth it.

ALDERFER/THREE SISTERS

DISTANCE:	Loop 1: 2.5 miles; Loop 2: 3.8 miles
ABILITY LEVEL:	Loop 1: Moderate II
	Loop 2: Easy II
TRAIL TYPE:	100% singletrack
CLIMBS:	Loop 1: Steep rocky ascents and descents
	Loop 2: One long, gradual climb 1st 2 miles
ELEVATION RANGE:	7,500-8,000 ft.
MAPS:	Pick up map at trailhead
DRIVING TIME FROM DENVER:	50 minutes

Do a double loop in Evergreen

Here are two different rides in one Jefferson County Park. Loop 1 is short, but it is definitely a Moderate II ride because of the rocky terrain and some short, steep climbs and switchbacks. Most of the rocks disappear on the trail in the most recent extension of the park, Evergreen Mtn. Trail East. But both have fantastic views of the entire Evergreen area and surrounding mountains and foothills.

GETTING THERE

Drive on I-70 west out of Denver and take the Evergreen/Colo. 74 exit. Follow Colo. 74 into town, past Elk Meadow Park and Evergreen Lake. On the edge of the downtown area, turn right onto Colo. 73. Take the next right onto Buffalo Park Road. Evergreen High School is on the left. The Alderfer/Three Sisters parking lot is .7 of a mile past the high school, on the right. (Note: Avoid entering or exiting this area during the time school is getting out for the day, between 2:30 and 3:30 p.m.)

ON THE TRAIL

Loop 1: Three Sisters and a Brother

"The Brother" and "Three Sisters" are rock outcroppings that have been landmarks for Evergreen residents since the first pioneers settled this area. A portion of the park was donated by the Alderfer family.

The first 0.4 of a mile is tough, but worth the view from the top. Follow the short leg of Ponderosa trail by taking the second left after entering the trail at the trailhead. Be careful climbing up several switchbacks amid scattered pine and aspen until 0.4, when the trail levels out. Keep following the Ponderosa trail to the left until you reach the Brothers Lookout trail. Follow it as it meanders for another 0.3 of a mile until it reaches some large boulders that mark the top of the this landmark called The Brother. The cyclist is treated to a commanding view of Evergreen and surrounding valleys and peaks, including Mt. Evans.

After a break here, start heading back down. Follow the Brothers Lookout trail back to the Ponderosa Trail and turn right to get onto the Sisters Trail. This part of the trail starts out fairly level at the top, but takes some healthy descents as you get closer to the junction with the Hidden Fawn Trail in less than a mile. Follow the Hidden Fawn as it continues to drop down to the parking lot via some switchbacks. There is a mixture of pine and aspen groves as you descend and the trail is extremely rocky in spots.

Loop 2: Evergreen East Trail

After you get to the parking lot and take a break, give this nice little loop a try.

The Evergreen East Trail and connecting trails are new additions to the Alderfer/ Three Sisters Park. This trail also has a good deal of climbing at the beginning and some great views at the top, but this is where their similarities end. Otherwise, you would think you drove to a different park. Virtually all of the Evergreen East Trail has a smooth surface with the exception of a couple of rocky spots here and there. Follow the signs for Evergreen East Trail. At the junction of the Ranch View Trail, stay on the Evergreen East Trail and go to your left.

From the trailhead to 1.3, the trail climbs steadily via many switchbacks but the trail surface is relatively rock-free. The steepest part is between 0.6 to 1.3. At 1.3, as the grade gets less severe, you begin to get some peeks of the valley below through the hundreds of tall pine trees around you. At about 1.4, the trail plunges into a "deep, dark forest" and comes out at 1.7 to broad daylight and a wonderful panoramic view of the valley below. Most of the remainder of the ride is a nice downhill run. Between 1.7 and 2.7, bike through a dense pine forest which is soon transformed into some nice meadows. At 3.1, you'll reach the wild Iris Loop trail. Stay on the Evergreen East Trail, go through a short, steep and winding downhill section, cross a maintained dirt road at 3.4 and go back to the parking lot.

WHILE YOU'RE THERE

On your way back home, check out Evergreen Lake. It has a hiking trail and sports a new log community building that's used for boat rentals in the summer and skating in the winter.

For more information on this area, see: **Jefferson County** *and the* **Colorado Tourism Board** *listings in the Recreational Resources section in the back of this book.*

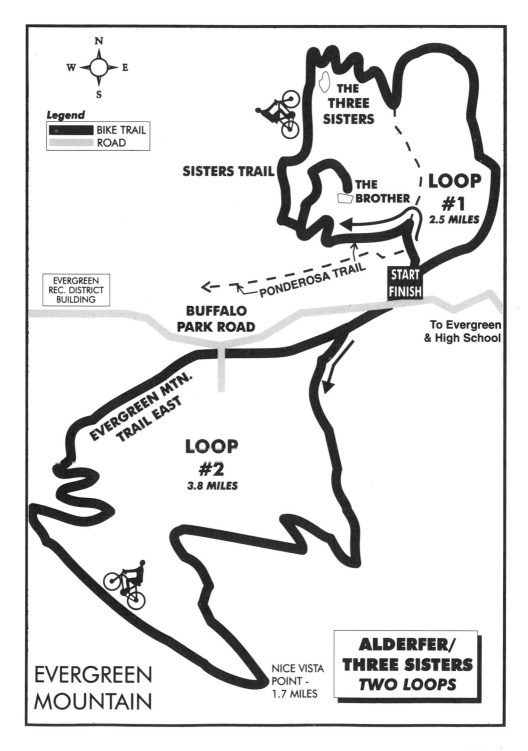

Legend
- ● ━━━ BIKE TRAIL
- ▓▓▓ ROAD

THE THREE SISTERS

SISTERS TRAIL

THE BROTHER

LOOP #1
2.5 MILES

EVERGREEN REC. DISTRICT BUILDING

PONDEROSA TRAIL

START FINISH

BUFFALO PARK ROAD

To Evergreen & High School

EVERGREEN MTN. TRAIL EAST

LOOP #2
3.8 MILES

EVERGREEN MOUNTAIN

NICE VISTA POINT - 1.7 MILES

ALDERFER/ THREE SISTERS
TWO LOOPS

BUFFALO CREEK

The rushing Buffalo Creek (right) is a welcome sight at the half-way point in the Buffalo Creek ride. On the way there, you'll experience some great views, such as the one below.

BUFFALO CREEK

DISTANCE:	15.8 miles roundtrip; shorter option
ABILITY RATING:	Moderate II entire trail;
	Easy II: shorter option
TRAIL TYPE:	100% singletrack
CLIMBS:	Several short climbs; one long
	climb on return
ELEVATION RANGE:	7,700-7,950 ft.
MAPS:	The Colorado Trail map; USFS: Pike
	National Forest; Trails Illustrated: No. 135
DRIVING TIME FROM DENVER:	1.25 hours

Take a smooth ride on a roller coaster

This portion of the Colorado Trail leading to Meadows Campground and Buffalo Creek (the creek, not the town) is in the Buffalo Creek Mountain Bike Area, part of the Pike National Forest southwest of Denver. Local mountain bikers have fallen in love with it. It offers the best of both worlds: It's challenging, but more importantly, fun, for all levels of riders. This portion of the trail has a remarkably smooth, rock-free surface on most of the route. To top it off, there are great vistas of the surrounding mountains and many unusual rock formations.

GETTING THERE

Drive on U.S. 285 south out of Denver to the town of Pine Junction, where you will turn left onto County Road 126. Follow this for 12 miles, past the tiny town of Buffalo Creek. Note the Colorado Trail parking lot (which often gets full) on your right at about 11.5 miles and drive .5 mile further to the next parking lot on the right side of the road. Park here.

ON THE TRAIL

After parking your car, find the signs to the Colorado Trail and the wooden fence you passed through to get there. Immediately, you will get the feeling of fun single-track riding: a smooth trail curving through the forest and enough ups and downs to give you that roller coaster feeling — and there are hardly any rocks in the trail to worry about.

In the first couple of miles, the trail curves through many stands of tall pines and sends you up and down a lot of small hills. Listen for the "soft crunch" of pine needles under your tires. You'll notice many unusual rock formations on either side of the trail and the constant smell of pine trees that surround you, providing that "deep woods" feeling.

At 2.0 miles, you're treated to a panoramic view of several peaks in the distance and a large rock formation that's more than 15 feet high.

After two short climbs at 2.5, you'll drop into a small deep valley with a large rock formation on the left. At 4.2, after riding over a high, sandy section of the trail, you'll reach another vista point with views of rock outcroppings and mountain peaks. At this point, beginners may consider turning back, because at 4.7, the trail takes a steady drop until 5.4, when it levels off a little, but it continues to descend until the end of the trail at 7.9. It's not that steep, just long.

Between 4.7 and 5.4, the trail goes through a nice grove of aspen. (For riders without bike computers, you will come to the longest descent yet in the ride, just after a nice vista point.)

In the last two miles before the Meadows Campground, there are entrances to three trail spurs, Green Mountain, Tramway, and Shinglemill. Many riders use these to turn this route into a great loop.

At the campground, there are picnic tables, an outhouse and a freshwater spigot with cold spring water during the summer months. While you're taking a break, follow the trail through the campground for .10 of a mile to the fast-running Buffalo Creek. Since you'll probably always refer to this area as "Buffalo Creek," you should at least look at its name sake. Return the same way you came.

SHORTER OPTION

You'll get the thrill of singletrack riding in the forest without the big hills and rocks by riding the first four miles of this trail and turning around.

WHILE YOU'RE THERE

There's a lot to explore in this area. Check out the several campgrounds and the many dirt roads. The Buffalo Creek Mountain Bike Area has about 40 miles of trails, and a lot of them are dirt roads. Only a small part of the Denver-to-Durango Colorado Trail goes through this area. When you get back to your car, note where the Colorado Trail crosses County Road 126. This is where another great mountain bike ride on this trail begins. See the Chair Rocks ride description in this book.

For additional information about this area, see: **South Platte Ranger District** *and the* **Buffalo Creek area** *listings in the Recreational Resources in the back of this book.*

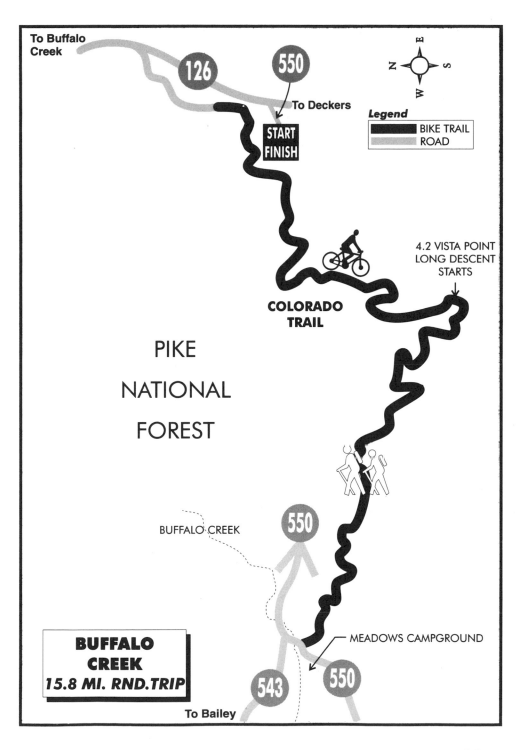

To Buffalo Creek

126

550

To Deckers

N E W S

Legend
BIKE TRAIL
ROAD

START FINISH

4.2 VISTA POINT LONG DESCENT STARTS

COLORADO TRAIL

PIKE

NATIONAL

FOREST

550

BUFFALO CREEK

MEADOWS CAMPGROUND

BUFFALO CREEK
15.8 MI. RND.TRIP

543

550

To Bailey

CHAIR ROCKS VIEWS

Massive rock formations called the Chair Rocks (above) and panoramic views await riders on this short-but-sweet singletrack ride through the Buffalo Creek Mountain Bike Area in the Pike National Forest.

CHAIR ROCKS

DISTANCE:	8.6 miles roundtrip
ABILITY LEVEL:	Easy II
TRAIL TYPE:	100 % singletrack
CLIMBS:	A few short climbs both ways
ELEVATION RANGE:	7,600-7,800 ft.
MAPS:	Trails Illustrated: No. 135; USFS: Pike National Forest; Colorado Trail map
DRIVING TIME FROM DENVER:	1.25 hours

These big rocks won't get in your way

This ride is definitely a lot of (visual) gain for the least pain (no big climbs). In this short ride, you'll experience some relatively smooth singletrack, and enjoy some great views of massive rock formations and some incredible peaks, including Pikes Peak. Beginners should have no problem with this ride.

GETTING THERE

Go south on U.S. 285 out of Denver to Pine Junction and turn left on the paved County Road 126. Drive about 11.5 miles, past the town of Buffalo, to the Colorado Trail parking lot on the right side of the road. Find the trail here and follow it across paved County Road 126.

ON THE TRAIL

After the trail crosses the road, it gradually descends for the first half-mile or so. It also curves quite a bit here, but the trail surface is generally smooth, similar to the Buffalo Creek trail across County Road 126.

The first climb of any consequence is at 0.7 and at 1.1, there's a rocky descent that some beginners may to want to walk through — it's only about a 200-foot stretch.

Just after this descent, look to your left. You'll get just a glimpse of the tops of the massive Chair Rocks. Hang on. You are about three miles away.

Most of this trail follows a ridge, which gives you a great vantage point to view some interesting rock formations and peaks to your right or south and southeast. At about 2.0, you'll be able to see Long Scraggy Peak to the southeast and Pikes Peak to the south.

Unfortunately, this trail does not go directly to the Chair Rocks, nor are there any signs to direct you there.

At the first maintained dirt road the trail crosses on this ride (at about **3.8**), turn left onto it. Ride on this road for no more than .2 of a mile and look for a drive-through dirt parking area on your right. Behind it is a fence with two "H" shaped log gates. Ride up to one of these and lift your bike over it (this type of gate was designed for this). You'll see an abandoned road bed that has been barricaded with piles of dirt and trees to discourage motor vehicles; don't take this. Take the trail that veers to the right. It is faint at first, but soon you'll see that you are on a bonafide trail. This trail curves delightfully through patches of dense forest for about .3 of a mile until you reach a clearing and the Chair Rocks. After you're done ogling at these monstrous rocks, walk a little further and you'll find something to match the rocks' grandeur: the view of numerous peaks to the west. With the *tops* of 25-foot pines at your feet in the foreground, you truly get the feeling you're airborne.

This makes a great spot to take a lunch break, play on the rocks or to just enjoy the view.

WHILE YOU'RE THERE:

About halfway to the Chair Rocks, keep your eye out for the Top of the World Campground. You might take a quick ride through it. This is one of the many campgrounds in the Mountain Bike Area of the Pike National Forest. If you still need more riding after you reach Chair Rocks, turn left onto the Colorado Trail from the first road you came down, instead of right, which will take you back to your car. You can sample as much of the trail as you can handle, but be warned: It steadily drops for several miles, which means a healthy climb coming back.

For more information on this area, see: **Buffalo Creek area** *and* **South Platte Ranger District** *in the Recreational Resources section in the back of this book.*

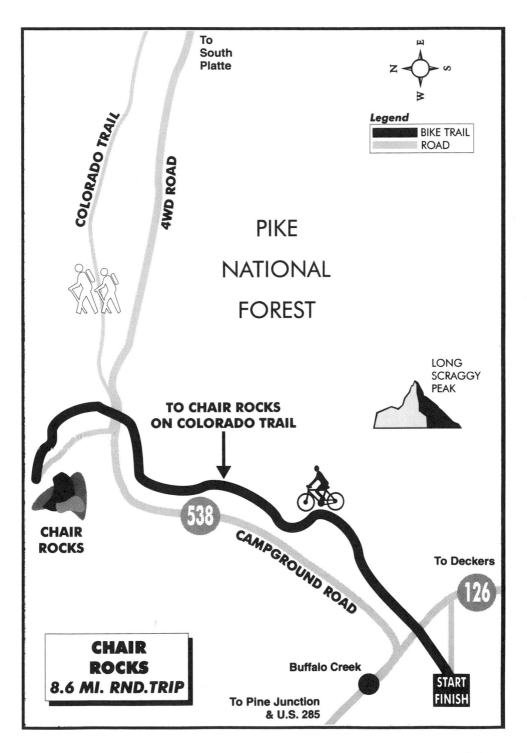

ELK MEADOW PARK

A bicycle rider takes a morning break to read the paper (above) in Evergreen's Elk Meadow Park, while another traverses the top of the meadow on this great little alpine ride close to Denver.

ELK MEADOW

DISTANCE:	5.6 miles — loop
ABILITY LEVEL:	Easy II
TRAIL TYPE:	100% singletrack
CLIMBS:	.5-mile climb 1st mile; few other short climbs
ELEVATION RANGE:	7,750-8,000 ft.
MAPS:	Get map at trailhead
DRIVING TIME FROM DENVER:	40 minutes

A cool mountain ride close to home

Hop in your car after work on a hot summer day and in about 40 minutes, you'll be transported to a cool, alpine retreat at Evergreen's Elk Meadow Park, another fine Jefferson County Park. This ride features cruises through dense stands of pine forest, panoramic views of Elk Meadow and a mixture of smooth and moderately rocky singletrack — an excellent ride for Easy II or Moderate I level riders.

GETTING THERE

Drive west on I-70 out of Denver and take the Evergreen/Colo. 74 exit. Drive on Colo. 74 toward Evergreen. One park entrance is on Colo. 74 two miles north of town. Another entrance, parking and picnic area is 1.25 miles west of Colo. 74 off of Stagecoach Blvd., near the top of the hill

ON THE TRAIL

You can start the ride from the parking lot on Colo. 74, or Stagecoach Blvd. parking lot. After starting from both places many times, I prefer starting in the lower parking lot off the highway.

Take a right out of the parking area onto the Painters Pause trail. You will soon take a left onto the Meadow View Trail. After about .3 of a mile of rolling meadow, you begin a steady climb that will transport you from mountain meadow to mountain forest.

There are a few mildly technical rocky sections on this climb, but overall, it's a fairly smooth trail. At the junction of the Meadow View and Too Long trails, at about 1.2, continue on the Meadow View Trail. It follows a long ridge that overlooks the meadow you just rode through. In the next half a mile or so, you will get some panoramic views of the meadows below as well as the Denver skyline in the distance.

From 1.5 to 3.7, the trail climbs gently but steadily, levels off and then starts dropping down. As you climb, you'll carve through "deep, dark forest" sections that will make you think you're 100 miles from Denver. As the trail drops, be careful with a couple of tricky switchbacks.

Elk Mountain is a very popular trail for both hikers and bikers; there's usually a 50/50 mix. On my many rides here, I've noticed that both hikers and bikers are extraordinarily courteous to each other. Let's all keep it that way.

At 3.7 is the junction with the Elkridge trail. Continue on the Meadow View Trail to the junction of the Sleepy S Trail. Enjoy this section of the ridge as you glide back to the meadow, traverse it and ride back to your car.

WHILE YOU'RE THERE

Because Elk Meadow Park is not that large, this is an excellent park for a group of hikers and bikers to enjoy at the same time. You can hike the entire perimeter of the route described here in two hours or less. There are several picnic tables near the Stagecoach Blvd. parking lot at the beginning of the trail there.

For a more challenging hike and a difficult/advanced mountain bike ride, go to the top of Bergen Peak (9,708 feet) on the Bergen Peak or Too Long Trail. This adds another 6.5 miles or so to the route described here, so be prepared. The Too Long Trail's many switchbacks take you through Denver Mountain Parks property, while the Bergen Peak Trail goes through the Bergen Peak Wildlife Area.

While you're in Evergreen, you might check out the Alderfer/Three Sisters Park across town. See the ride description in this book.

For more information on this area, see: **Jefferson County (West Chamber of Commerce and Jefferson County Open Space)** *and the* **Colorado Tourism Board** *in the Recreational Resources section in the back of this book.*

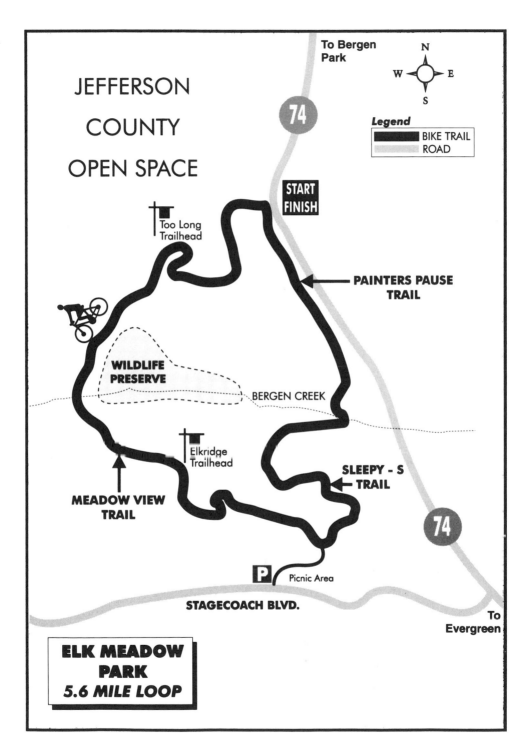

JEFFERSON
COUNTY
OPEN SPACE

To Bergen Park

74

Legend
BIKE TRAIL
ROAD

N
W E
S

START
FINISH

Too Long Trailhead

PAINTERS PAUSE TRAIL

WILDLIFE PRESERVE

BERGEN CREEK

Elkridge Trailhead

SLEEPY - S TRAIL

MEADOW VIEW TRAIL

74

P Picnic Area

STAGECOACH BLVD.

To Evergreen

ELK MEADOW PARK
5.6 MILE LOOP

FLUME TRAIL SERENITY
Serene scenes like these are common along the peaceful Flume Trail near Fraser and Winter Park.

THE FLUME TRAIL

DISTANCE: 5.1 miles -- Loop
ABILITY LEVEL: Easy II
Suitable for children
TRAIL TYPE: 100% single/doubletrack
CLIMBS: Few short climbs in first two miles
ELEVATION RANGE: 8,830-9,000 ft.
MAPS: USFS: Arapaho & Roosevelt National Forests
Trails Illustrated: No. 501, Winter Park
DRIVING TIME FROM DENVER: 1.5 hours

Bike into a serene forest on Flume Trail

After 30 minutes of riding this route, you feel as though you've been submerged into a forest miles from nowhere. Actually, this trail is just a couple of miles from the town of Fraser and has become one of the locals' favorites because of the "deep woods" feeling and easy pedaling.

GETTING THERE
The trickiest thing about this ride is *finding* it. As you come into Fraser from Winter Park on U.S. 40, look for Eisenhower Ave. on your left. Follow this road as it turns to the left and joins with County Road 73, which you will turn right onto. Take CR 73 for 2.5 miles to the St. Louis Creek Campground. Turn left onto the campground access road and park in the large turnoff on the right side of this road just before the campground gate. You can start your bike ride from the town of Fraser and ride CR 73 out to the campground and pick up the trail. I decided to start and finish at the campground to make this a short and sweet 100 percent double/singletrack trail ride.

ON THE TRAIL
Look for the trailhead sign for the Creekside Trail on the left of the campground access road, just before the gate. Start riding on the side of the road opposite this sign. The trail — an abandoned roadbed at this point — is very faint at first but will become more apparent after a minute or two of riding. The trail parallels St. Louis Creek for about two miles. It can be very rocky in spots, but the grade is gentle. Beginners or small children may have to walk parts of this section.

Take a break along the creek before turning left onto CR 159 at about two miles. Ride on the road for .1 of a mile to cross the creek, then turn left onto the Flume Trail. In minutes, you'll be transported to mountain biker's utopia: a smooth, almost soft, trail beneath your tires as you are surrounded by the hush of tall lodgepole pines, occasional meadows and small streams for the next couple of miles -- and no big hills, either.

Take a minute in one of the small mountain meadows or stands of lodgepole pines or aspen groves to enjoy the serenity here. At 3.9, you'll reach a low, boggy area that may require some puddle jumping. Try to avoid making any further ruts on or off the trail. Also in this area, you'll get a good view of the surrounding mountain ranges through the trees. At about 4.3, you'll reach the junction of Chainsaw Trail (which would take you back to town) and the campground cutoff. Take the campground trail to your left and soon you'll be crossing the creek again. Immediately (no more than 10 feet) after crossing the creek turn left and pick up the Creekside Trail. This will take you back to the campground.

WHILE YOU'RE THERE

Camping at the St. Louis Creek Campground would be a convenient way to sample the trails in this area. Small children should be able to handle the Flume Trail, but they may have to walk parts of the Creekside Trail. If you're looking for more recreational diversity, Rocky Mountain National Park and Colorado's largest natural lake, Grand Lake, is less than an hour's drive from Fraser up the valley. (Mountain biking is not permitted on the park's hiking trails.)

For more information on this area, see: **Winter Park/Grand County** *listings in the Recreational Resources section in the back of this book.*

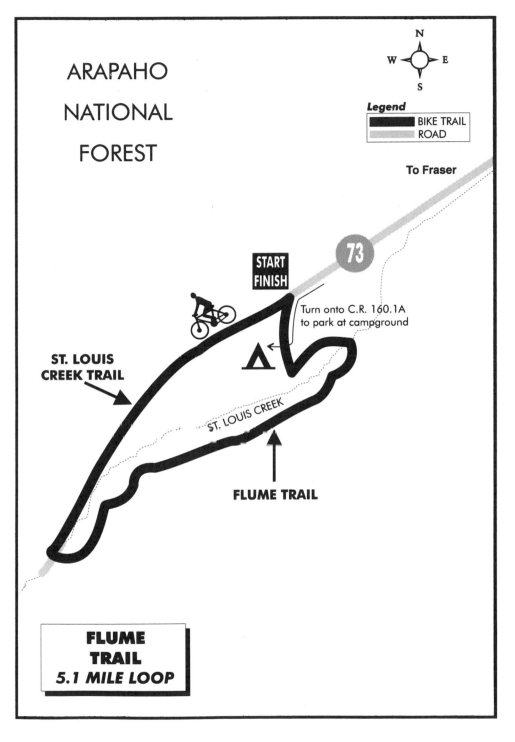

ARAPAHO NATIONAL FOREST

Legend
BIKE TRAIL
ROAD

To Fraser

73

START FINISH

Turn onto C.R. 160.1A to park at campground

ST. LOUIS CREEK TRAIL

ST. LOUIS CREEK

FLUME TRAIL

FLUME TRAIL 5.1 MILE LOOP

GREEN MOUNTAIN PARK

Yes, this is 30 minutes from Denver, although it looks like scenes from Southwestern Colorado. The red rocks and smooth trails (right), sweeping foothills views and unusual rock formations in the Green Mountain park make this a fun mountain bike escape close to Denver.

GREEN MOUNTAIN

DISTANCE: 6.9 miles — loop
ABILITY LEVEL: Easy I first half; Easy II entire loop
TRAIL TYPE: 80% singletrack; 20% doubletrack
CLIMBS: One short climb 1st half;
One 0.7-mile climb 2nd half
ELEVATION RANGE: 6,200-6,800 ft. (Green Mt. summit)
MAPS: Lakewood Non-Motorized Trail Guide
(Call: City of Lakewood, 303-987-7800)
DRIVING TIME FROM DENVER: 25 minutes

View red rocks, foothills, city skyline

The Green Mountain Trail is a wonderful ride, less than a 30-minute drive from downtown Denver. The combination of singletrack and abandoned dirt roads, some easy technical sections and views of the downtown Denver skyline and the surrounding foothills make this an ideal ride for the beginner/intermediate rider.

GETTING THERE

From Denver, drive on I-70 west and take the Morrison exit. Follow Colo. 26 under I-70 for 1.5 miles to the intersection with Colo. 26 east. Turn left here and drive on this until you reach Rooney Road at the bottom of a large hill. Turn left here and drive .6 of a mile to the Green Mountain parking lot.

ON THE TRAIL

From the parking lot, start riding uphill and go to the right on the singletrack trail that goes in between two small hills. After a short, steep climb, you will be climbing fairly gradually along a ridge for the next few miles.

The first few miles of this trail give you great views of the rolling meadows and the foothills to your right. At about 1.0, you get a view of the mammoth red rocks that form Red Rocks Park and amphitheater across the valley to the west. As the trail gently climbs and winds along the ridge, you get different angles of your view of the valley and various red rock formations. Most of this part of the trail is very smooth, with only a couple of rocky sections. At certain spots in the trail, you'll see small clumps of housing developments in the distance. Thanks to the foresight of urban planners, we have open-space "islands" such as this one so close to the cities.

Speaking of cities, at 3.4, you get an excellent view of the downtown Denver sky-line to the east — if the smog isn't too bad. Also at this point, you can see the park's second parking lot at the bottom of a steep hill. If you are a beginning rider who is still uncomfortable with rocky riding and steeper climbs, this might be a good place to turn around. By turning around, your ride will be almost exactly the same length as the entire loop and you'll still get a good taste of singletrack riding.

If you want to continue, here's what you'll find. After going down and through the second parking lot, pick up the trail and start climbing, at 4.0. This is the longest and steepest climb of the ride so far. It also has several rocky sections to negotiate. At 4.7, you finally reach the top of Green Mountain and you are rewarded for your work with some fantastic views of mountain peaks and rolling meadows in front of you. Although you are far from it, the peak has an above-timberline feeling to it.

After following the rolling trail along the top of the mountain, at 6.0, shoot down-hill until you reach your car at 6.9.

WHILE YOU'RE THERE

On your way back to Interstate 70, check out Matthews/Winters Park (see the ride description in this book) park on your left, just before getting back onto the high-way. If you turn left onto Colo. 26 instead of right toward I-70, you can go to Red Rocks Park. While its amphitheater is famous for the concerts and sunrise Easter services held there, it is also a popular hiking and biking area.

*For additional information about this area, see: **Jefferson County (West Chamber of Commerce)** and the **Colorado Tourism Board** in the Recreational Resources section of this book.*

KENOSHA PASS ON THE COLORADO TRAIL
Riders weave through an aspen grove in the fall on the smooth Colorado Trail over Kenosha Pass. This section of the trail offers ideal singletrack riding and some fantastic scenery — especially in the fall.

KENOSHA PASS

DISTANCE:	16.2 miles roundtrip
ABILITY LEVEL:	Moderate II entire route; Easy II 1st half
TRAIL TYPE:	100% singletrack
CLIMBS:	Strenuous climb in last 2 miles to lunch rock; long gradual climb on return
ELEVATION RANGE:	10,00-10,800 ft.
MAPS:	USFS: Pike National Forest; USGS 7.5: Jefferson, Boreas Pass; Colorado Trail map
DRIVING TIME FROM DENVER:	1.25 hours

Kenosha Pass: Singletrack heaven

This beautiful ride through aspen groves, a spectacular mountain valley and up and down one of central Colorado's prettiest mountain passes is known by experienced riders as the grueling 12-mile route (24 roundtrip) to Georgia Pass. But it doesn't have to be that way for you. The most scenic, enjoyable — and the easiest — part of this section of the Colorado Trail is the first five miles. In fact, beginning riders can get the feeling of a singletrack high-country ride with a four-mile roundtrip jaunt and enjoy some of the best views of the trip. Level II moderate riders who want more of a challenge can climb part of the way to Georgia Pass and get another great view from the other side of the valley.

GETTING THERE

Drive south on U.S. 285 out of Denver to Kenosha Pass and turn right at the top of the pass into the parking area just outside of the campground.

ON THE TRAIL

Start riding up the road to the Kenosha Pass Campground and follow the signs for the Colorado Trail.

The ride starts out with a short climb, then a long descent into the valley to Jefferson Creek and then a two-mile climb to a lookout point called lunch rock, which is where I ended this ride and turned back for a 16.2-mile roundtrip.

The first climb brings you through the campground and into a dense pine forest for 1.1 miles. The gradual ascent was more than worth it. You are treated to a sweeping view of the entire valley and South Park, a large expanse of open meadows dotted with aspen and pine groves. In the fall, when the aspen are changing color, you just want to get off your bike and marvel at it for a while.

Continue on the trail as it slowly drops into the valley on the west side of the pass. Because this area is so open, beginners can judge their point to turn around.

For the next 1.5 miles, there are several natural pulloffs from the trail, making it easy to enjoy the view below. Almost every stop gives you a different perspective on the valley and peaks beyond.

At 3.5, begin going through a large meadow punctuated by aspen groves. Between 3.5 and 4.5, start a slow, steady climb out of the valley through some aspen and pine stands. There is a short climb to get to the 5-mile point in your journey, but you are rewarded with a great view of the valley floor you just crossed. Just after 5.0, you encounter the rockiest section of the trail so far. Up until this point, the trail is exceptionally smooth, the ideal singletrack trail. After a short climb, start dropping down to the Jefferson Creek. The trail crosses a maintained dirt road, Jefferson Lake Road, at 6.0 and a tenth of a mile later, you reach Jefferson Creek and the half-way point to Georgia Pass.

Level II beginners should be able to handle the ride to this point and it wouldn't be a bad place to turn around.

The next two miles are mostly *up*, via some very rocky trail surfaces and many switchbacks. By taking it easy, most intermediates won't have any problem. In this section, it would be nice to have a bike computer, because the 2.1 miles to the lunch rock viewing area seem to take forever when you're constantly climbing. You will be climbing through a fairly densely forested area.

The first real break in the trees that gives you a view of the valley is the lunch rock stop. You can see Jefferson Lake and Glacier and Whale peaks to the north.

The trail continues for four more miles to Georgia Pass, but it is as difficult or more difficult as the 2-mile climb you just did. After a break, return the way you came.

WHILE YOU'RE THERE

Check out the Kenosha Pass Campground for a possible stay there or cross U.S. 285 and hike the Colorado Trail there. (People do bike it, but it's a more difficult/ advanced ride.) Instead of going back to Denver on U.S. 285, drive toward Fairplay and take the Boreas Pass road into Breckenridge. It's a dirt road, but in the summer, it can accommodate 2-wheel-drive cars and the views are great on top of the pass. In Fairplay, history buffs may be interested in South Park City, a restored "Old West" town.

For more information on this area, see: **Buffalo Creek area, Park County** *in the Recreational Resources section in the back of this book.*

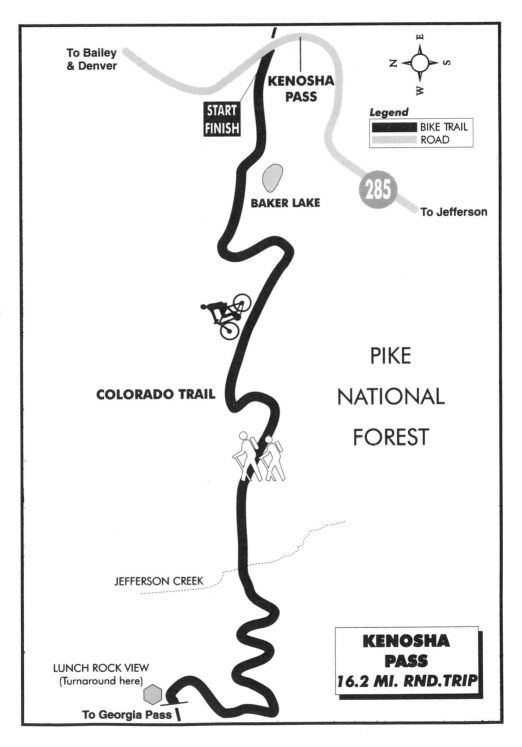

To Bailey & Denver

KENOSHA PASS

START FINISH

Legend
BIKE TRAIL
ROAD

285

To Jefferson

BAKER LAKE

PIKE

NATIONAL

FOREST

COLORADO TRAIL

JEFFERSON CREEK

KENOSHA PASS
16.2 MI. RND. TRIP

LUNCH ROCK VIEW
(Turnaround here)

To Georgia Pass

MATTHEWS/WINTERS PARK

A lone rider (right) makes his way up the Red Rocks Trail, which connects Red Rocks Park with Matthews/Winters Park. The park is filled with deep red rocks, dry terrain and other desert-like scenes. It also offers the rider some sweeping views of the foothills and plains (below).

MATTHEWS/WINTERS PARK

DISTANCE: 5.2 miles — loop
ABILITY LEVEL: Moderate II: full loop; Easy II: easier option
TRAIL TYPE: 100% singletrack
CLIMBS: One long climb on Morrison Slide Trail
ELEVATION RANGE: 6,400-6,800 ft.
MAPS: Pick up trail map at trailhead
DRIVING TIME FROM DENVER: 20-30 minutes

Ride through the red rocks, foothills

This is a great ride for beginners or intermediates who want to practice riding skills close to the Denver area while still getting out of town and enjoying some views of red rock formations, the surrounding foothills and lakes in the distance.

The first loop described here is for Moderate II riders because of the many rocky sections and switchbacks. However, I also make a recommendation for Easy II riders.

GETTING THERE

Drive west on I-70 to the Morrison exit. Follow Colo. 26 under the highway and start looking to your right for the sign for Matthews/Winters park; it's about .3 of a mile from the highway exit. Park in the parking lot at the park.

ON THE TRAIL

On this loop, always go to the right on the way out and stay to the right on the way back. After a short climb on the Village Walk Trail, the trail levels out until you reach the Red Rocks Trail at 0.3. For the next half-mile, the trail climbs steadily using some switchbacks. There are some rocky sections, but overall, the Red Rocks Trail is not that tough. Turn right onto the Morrison Slide Trail at 1.0. This is where the steep climbs and switchbacks begin, accompanied by some tricky rocky sections.

Beginners and some intermediates will want to walk many sections here — but it won't last that long. At about 1.4, you receive your visual reward when you reach the top of a plateau. Take a break and enjoy the views in every direction, especially the foothills and reservoirs in the distance to the south and southwest. You'll enjoy some level riding as the trail curves across the top of the mesa for another half a mile or so and then drops down via some fairly steep switchbacks to the junction of the Red Rocks Trail. You can take the spur trail to Red Rocks Park, but you'll notice it goes *down*.

Turn *left* onto the Red Rocks trail, climb for about .10 of a mile, and most of the remainder of the 2.4 miles back to the car is a cruise with only a few short climbs, which brings me to the easy way out — and back.

EASIER OPTION

Instead of turning on the Morrison Slide Trail at 1.0, continue on the Red Rocks Trail, using the return leg of this loop. Ride to the three-way junction of the Red Rocks and Morrison Slide Trails and turn around. You'll still get some pretty views of the foothills, mountains, valleys and red rock formations, without all the climbing in the loop described above — and you'll ride almost the same mileage.

WHILE YOU'RE THERE

After your ride, take a look at Dakota Ridge Trail across Colo. 26. The trail follows a high rocky (rocky is the key word here) ridge that more experienced/advanced bike riders use to make a loop out of the trails you just rode on. However, a hike in this area is also interesting. There are several interpretive signs at the base of the ridge that explain the history of rock formations and dinosaurs between 120 million and 140 million years ago. Dinosaur remains were first found on the "Dakota Hogback" in 1877, and in late 1920s, dinosaur footprints were found on the ridge. In late 1993, plans were being made to refurbish an older house and barn for use as a visitor center. On school days, you'll see busloads of students exploring the rocks.

For more information on this area, see: **Colorado Tourism Board** *and* **Jefferson County** *listings in the Recreational Resources section in the back of this book.*

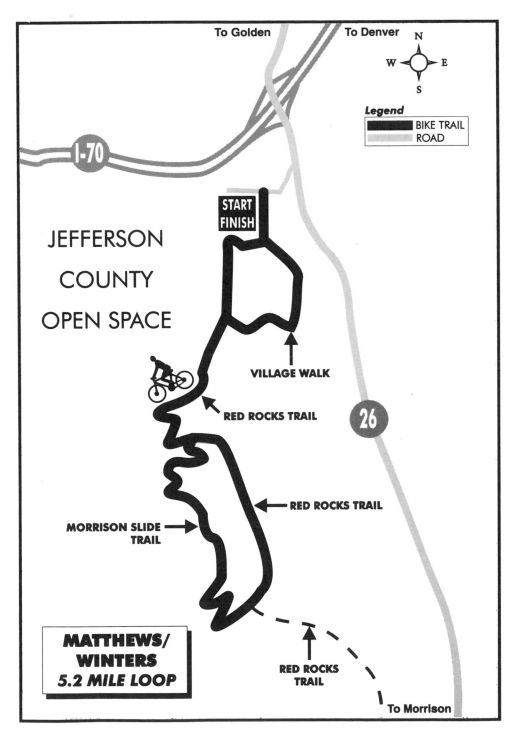

To Golden

To Denver

N
W — E
S

Legend
BIKE TRAIL
ROAD

I-70

START FINISH

JEFFERSON
COUNTY
OPEN SPACE

VILLAGE WALK

RED ROCKS TRAIL

26

RED ROCKS TRAIL

MORRISON SLIDE TRAIL

MATTHEWS/ WINTERS
5.2 MILE LOOP

RED ROCKS TRAIL

To Morrison

SWITZERLAND TRAIL

Mark Dowling (below), author of *Bike With a View*, makes his way down the Switzerland Trail west of Boulder. The trail follows an old railway bed and offers mountain views. (Photo by Saundra Dowling)

SWITZERLAND TRAIL

DISTANCE:	11.0 miles roundtrip
ABILITY LEVEL:	Easy I
TRAIL TYPE:	100% abandoned dirt road
CLIMBS:	Gentle climb first half; cruise back
ELEVATION RANGE:	8,500-9,000 ft.
MAPS:	Trails Illustrated No.102 Indian Peaks
	USFS: Roosevelt National Forest
DRIVING TIME FROM DENVER:	1 hour

Take the high road, enjoy the views

The Switzerland Trail is one of the most popular mountain bike rides in the Boulder area for good reason. This abandoned railway bed transports the rider to some wonderful mountain views in every direction. The 5.5-mile portion of the trail to Glacier Lake is great for beginners. It has very gentle grades and is just rocky enough in spots to remind you that you're on a *real* mountain bike ride!

GETTING THERE

From Broadway in Boulder, take Canyon Road (Colo. Highway 119) west 5.5 miles. Right after going through a tunnel, turn right on Sugarloaf Road. Follow this very steep road to Sugarloaf Mountain Road and take this for one more mile to the trailhead and parking area.

ON THE TRAIL

The parking area for the Switzerland Trail is the Grand Central Station of mountain bike routes: There seem to be trails and roads coming in from every direction. Start riding on the trail that is marked with the sign "Glacier Lake." It forks to the left when you're facing the sign. (It's also the most popular — follow the crowd!)

The trail is mildly rocky in spots, so beginners should be careful. Almost immediately, you'll get some nice mountain vistas to your left of the surrounding mountains, valleys and foothills that are worth stopping for. Thousands of cyclists have worn down their favorite portions of the roadway, creating a sort of singletrack trail on the roadbed.

For most of the first half of the ride out (about 5 of the 5.5 miles), you'll be going uphill, but the grade is gradual; the trail is an abandoned railroad bed. A narrow gauge train rumbled across the soil you're riding on in the late 1800s and hauled gold ore from the Sugarloaf and Gold Hill mines to Boulder. The railroad was abandoned in the early 1900s after the mines shut down. The trail passes through a few fairly thickly forested areas, but most of the route follows a high ridge, allowing riders to see the forest from the trees and take in some great mountain vistas on both sides of the trail.

You will see riders of varying abilities, bikes and ages, but because bikers and hikers have the entire width of the trail, it is rarely so jammed that riding is uncomfortable. When I rode the trail, I saw small children, mountain bikers racing each other to the top, a horseback rider and a man on an old touring bike (not recommended).

At about 5 miles, you'll see the "no trespassing" signs and fences that mark Glacier Lake. While this is technically a ride to Glacier Lake, you never get to see it because it is now private and is fenced off. No matter, the other views and easy trail are well worth the ride. The trail levels out here. You can ride a little further to Colo. 72, the Peak to Peak Highway (to get the full 11 miles roundtrip in) or just turn around here.

The mostly downhill cruise back to the car will give beginners excellent practice on negotiating rocky sections at a steady speed.

WHILE YOU'RE THERE

If you're still eager to go, you might try the other portion of the Switzerland trail that goes down and to the right to the old mining town of Sunset. This is a much longer ride than the Glacier Lake route and you know what going *down* means!

If you're new to the area or a visitor, try the many fine paved bike trails in the City of Boulder. Boulder is a biker's heaven. A warning, however: Avoid riding on the Canyon Road (Colo. 119) after the bike path ends. (You'll see the bike path on the drive up to Sugarloaf.) There have been some serious bike/car accidents on this road to Nederland.

If you want to drive to Nederland, you'll find a funky little mountain community of new and preserved mountain cabins and small businesses. A favorite restaurant for the many hikers, skiers and bicyclists that descend on the town during the weekends is Neopolitan's (known as "Neo's"). It's famous for its Italian dishes, especially the calzones and pizzas.

For more information on this area, see: **Denver-Boulder area** *in the Recreational Resources section in the back of this book.*

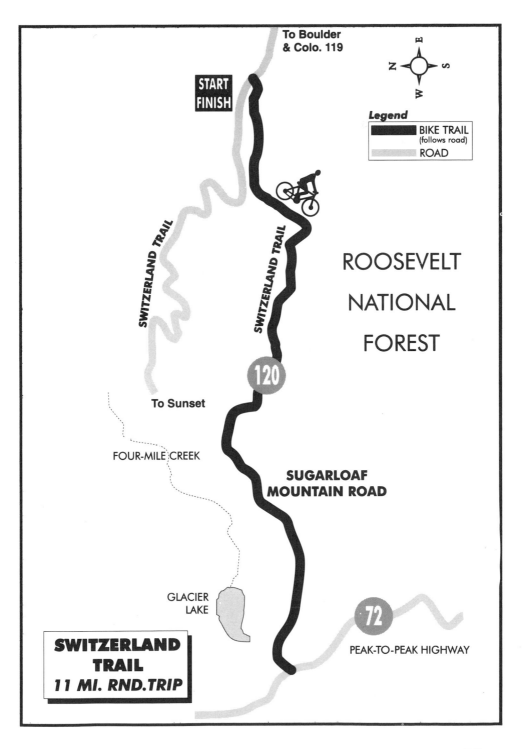

To Boulder
& Colo. 119

START
FINISH

N E S W

Legend

BIKE TRAIL
(follows road)
ROAD

SWITZERLAND TRAIL

SWITZERLAND TRAIL

ROOSEVELT

NATIONAL

FOREST

120

To Sunset

FOUR-MILE CREEK

SUGARLOAF
MOUNTAIN ROAD

GLACIER
LAKE

72

PEAK-TO-PEAK HIGHWAY

SWITZERLAND
TRAIL
11 MI. RND.TRIP

BIKING OASES

Colorado is hardly overflowing with water.

Millions of gallons of water have to be constantly dumped on lawns and gardens to keep them alive and the state averages about 14 inches of precipitation a year.

But the water Colorado state does have is special: high-mountain lakes nestled in the pines and rivers that eventually make their way to two oceans on both sides of the Continental Divide.

Virtually every major "lake" along Colorado's Front Range is a reservoir. These man-made bodies of water are necessary to feed a growing population, thousands of acres of crops and livestock herds.

The eastern-flowing rivers that feed these reservoirs don't supply enough water, how-ever, to satisfy this huge thirst in an arid area. Billions of gallons of water annually are "injected" into eastern-flowing rivers via some sophisticated engineering hijinks called "water diversion projects."

One of the positive side effects of these projects is the recreational opportunities these waters create for boaters, swimmers, fishers or anyone who just wants to ride or hike around a lake.

A perfect example of this dual role that water plays in Colorado is the giant Dillon Reservoir in Summit County. The reservoir was completed in 1963 by flooding the former town site of Dillon. The water from the western-flowing Blue River is stored here and diverted *under* the Continental Divide into the North Fork of the South Platte River via the Roberts Tunnel. At the time, the reservoir more than doubled Denver's water supply and still is the city's major water source.

Dillon Reservoir's 256 miles of shoreline offer water-lovers many recreational adven-tures, from motor boating and sailing to fishing, hiking and biking.

As you bike around the lakes or along the South Platte River (Waterton Canyon) de-scribed in this section, remember that the water that you're dipping your feet into or watching fade with the sunset will also probably end up in your garden, lawn or bath-tub.

BLUE LAKES
One of the Blue Lakes near Breckenridge and Hoosier Pass sits among some high peaks. The dirt road to the Blue Lakes is good practice for Easy II and Moderate riders.

BLUE LAKES

DISTANCE:	4.2 miles roundtrip
ABILITY LEVEL:	Easy II
TRAIL TYPE:	100% dirt road
CLIMBS:	Long, gradual climb to lakes
ELEVATION RANGE:	10,850-11,680 ft.
MAPS:	USGS: 7.5 Breckenridge; Trails Illustrated: No. 109; USFS: Arapaho National Forest, Dillon Ranger District
DRIVING TIME FROM DENVER:	1.5 hours

You're surrounded by peaks, lakes

This short Easy II ride will give you an opportunity to build your mountain bike handling skills and climbing stamina on a moderately rocky dirt road while pedaling up to two small lakes nestled among massive rocky peaks in the high country.

GETTING THERE

Drive about 7.5 miles south of Brekenridge on Colo. 9 toward Hoosier Pass. Turn right onto County Road 850, also known as Blue Lakes Road. Continue on CR 850, .2 of a mile past the Blue Lakes sign (at the intersection of CR 851) and park in the large turnout on the right side of the road.

ON THE TRAIL

Most of the first half of this ride is uphill, but the scenery will take your mind off the pedaling. The climbs are not very steep, but if you're a beginner, they can tend to seem long, especially because of the elevation of this ride, which is between about 10,850 feet and 11,680 feet above sea level.

Follow the road as it winds its way to the lakes. Although this ride is easy, there are some fairly rocky sections along the way. Two-wheel drive cars travel this road, but traffic is very light to nonexistent.

On the way to the lakes, start noticing some of the highest peaks in this area of the state looming above you, including Quandary Peak (14,265 feet) to the right on your way up. As you reach the area between the two small lakes (at 1.8), the envelope of mountains you have been riding through is almost complete.

Look down toward the direction you came from and enjoy the view of the small lake at your feet and the rocky peaks surrounding you. Now take a quick jaunt down to the base of the second lake and a short, steep climb to the paved surface of the dam in front of the second lake.

You'll enjoy a view of the second lake and yet another vantage point to gaze at more peaks behind it. Return the same way you came.

WHILE YOU'RE THERE

If you're still aching for some more miles under your knobbies, turn right at the Blue Lakes sign, and take County Road 851 up the hill. Several dirt roads meander through this area, but you should have a map if you're going to do any extensive riding.

Instead of heading back to Breckenridge after your ride, take a right onto Colo. 9 instead of a left and drive on it for about 15 minutes up to the top of Hoosier Pass and enjoy the view. If you're heading back to Denver, keep driving south on Colo. 9 to hook up with Colo. 285 at Fairplay. If you're in the historic mood, take a quick tour of South Park City, a replica of an old-west town.

On the way back to Denver from Fairplay, take a quick break at Kenosha Pass and maybe even sample the beginning of the Kenosha Pass ride described in this book.

For more information on this area, see: **Summit County** *and* **Buffalo Creek area, Park County** *listings in the Recreational Resources in the back of this book.*

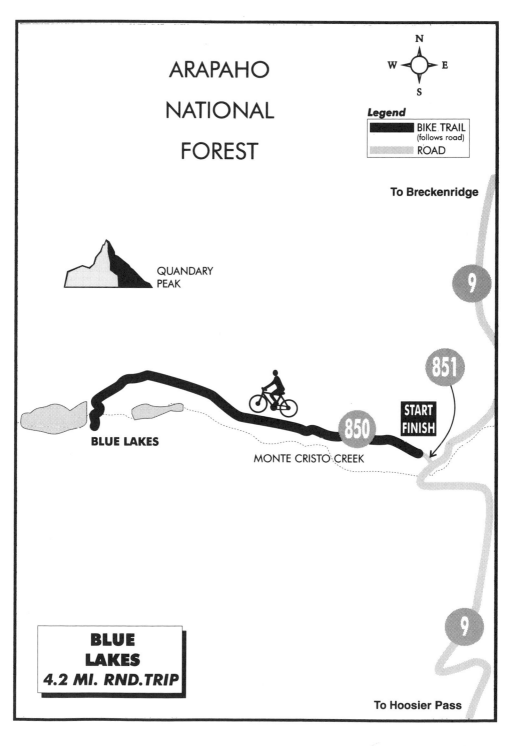

ARAPAHO

NATIONAL

FOREST

N
W · E
S

Legend
BIKE TRAIL (follows road)
ROAD

To Breckenridge

9

QUANDARY PEAK

851

850

START FINISH

BLUE LAKES

MONTE CRISTO CREEK

9

BLUE LAKES
4.2 MI. RND.TRIP

To Hoosier Pass

DILLON RESERVOIR

An abandoned dirt road (right) takes bicyclists to Dillon Reservoir's Crown Point beach. It's a great place for a picnic and the route is for all levels of riders.

DILLON RESERVOIR

DISTANCE:	5.0 miles roundtrip
ABILITY LEVEL:	Easy I
	Suitable for young children
TRAIL TYPE:	90% doubletrack; 10% easy singletrack
CLIMBS:	Minimal; 1 short climb each way
ELEVATION RANGE:	9,050-9,240 ft.
MAPS:	USFS: Arapaho National Forest, Dillon
	Trails Illustrated: No.108, Vail/Frisco/Dillon
DRIVING TIME FROM DENVER:	1.75 hours

An easy bike ride to the lake shore

This is a great ride for all abilities and ages with a fun destination: the lake shore of Dillon Reservoir. It's an easy ride on abandoned dirt roads with just enough singletrack to give children of *all* ages some excitement.

GETTING THERE

Drive south on Colo. 9 past Frisco. Look for the Arapaho National Forest sign on the left side of the road that reads: "Forest Recreation Area /Peninsula /Peak One/ Pine Cove." Turn left here and drive in a short way until you see a large parking lot, restrooms and a day-use area on the right. Park here.

ON THE TRAIL

Follow the paved road to the right, toward the campground. Take a right at the first dirt road that intersects the paved road. Ride on this until you come to a gate. Lift your bike through it and continue.

The trail is an easy abandoned dirt road that climbs very gradually and starts turning left and heading down towards Dillon Reservoir at about 1.5 miles.

At about 1.8 miles, you will start seeing just a little piece of the huge reservoir as you drop toward it. On either side of the trail, 25-foot pines tower over you. Even though you can't see it, you are actually riding on a large peninsula of the lake.

At 2.2, the road will start to turn into a circle to the left. Just as it starts to turn, look for the beginning of an unmarked singletrack trail that goes down the hill to the right. If you have children riding with you — especially boys — they'll find it like bloodhounds and start racing down it well ahead of you!

This .3-mile singletrack drops into the woods and brings you out to the lake shore at Crown Point. It has a nice sandy beach and a great view of Dillon Reservoir and the Continental Divide peaks beyond. This would be a great place for a picnic lunch or a snack.

WHILE YOU'RE THERE

Check out the several campgrounds and boat launching areas that are on every side of the reservoir. This trail starts near two of the campgrounds, Peak One and Pine Cove. This the largest reservoir closest to Denver. There's plenty of room for sailers, motor boats and fishermen. If you're a (paved) road biker, you might look into cycling around the reservoir via the Dillon-Frisco trail and Swan Mountain Road, which does a healthy climb over Swan Mountain.

There are many other opportunities for some road biking while you're in Summit County. The Blue River Bikeway is a dedicated bike/hike paved trail (*not* a road shoulder!) that parallels Colo. 9 and the Blue River between Breckenridge and Frisco. It's a gentle grade and an excellent example of how a bike trail can work as a recreation trail *and* a practical transportation route; many locals use the trail regularly to get from one town to another. If you (or someone in your party) are extremely energetic, continue following this bike trail as it goes past the Copper Mountain Ski Area and changes to the Vail Pass trail. You'll probably need a day to go to Vail and back comfortably, but it's probably one of the easiest and most pleasant mountain pass climbs by bike you'll find in the state.

For more information on this area, see: **Summit County** *listings in the Recreational Resources section in the back of this book.*

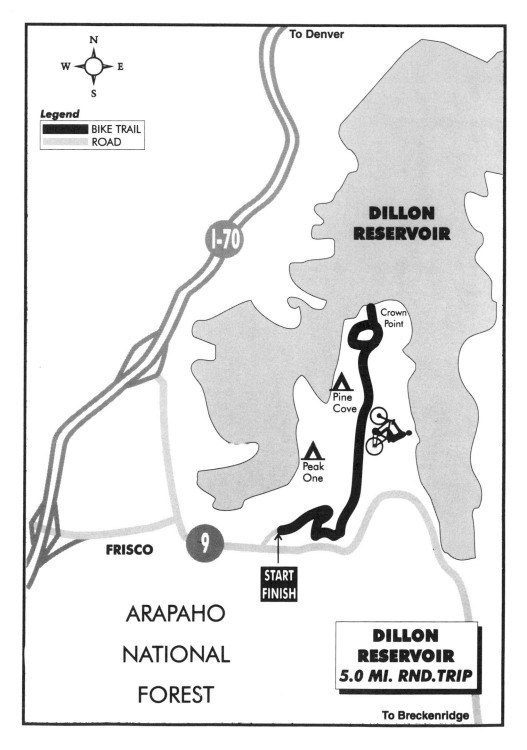

DOWDY LAKE
Dowdy Lake is one of the Red Feather Lakes in northern Colorado. Besides going to the lake, you can also bike to Mt. Margaret on this trail.

DOWDY LAKE

DISTANCE:	9.4 miles — loop
ABILITY LEVEL:	Easy I
TRAIL TYPE:	100% singletrack/doubletrack
CLIMBS:	Few short climbs; one longer climb to lake
ELEVATION RANGE:	7,900-8,040 ft.
MAPS:	USFS: Roosevelt, Arapaho National Forests; Trails Illustrated: No. 111, Red Feather Lakes
DRIVING TIME FROM DENVER:	2 hours

Bike to a lake, climb a mountain

This is a great easy ride for the family. You'll visit a mountain lake with sandy beaches, ride a dirt road through an *active* cow pasture and "climb" to a mountain peak in 30 seconds!

GETTING THERE

Take I-25 north to the U.S. 14 west/ U.S. 287 north exit. Weave your way through Fort Collins following the 287/north signs until you get to the tiny crossroads town of Livermore and County Road 74E. This is also called the Red Feather Lakes Road. Drive 21 miles west until you reach the Mt. Margaret trailhead on the right.

ON THE TRAIL

This is actually called the Mt. Margaret trail, but taking the side trail to Dowdy Lake on the way back makes a great loop and good place for a break, lunch or a swim!

The Mt. Margaret trail meanders through some grazing pastures, past some interesting rock formations and climaxes with a single track section that leads to Mt. Margaret, affording some magnificent views of the surrounding peaks and fields.

There are no extended climbs on the entire route, which makes for a good introduction to singletrack and "doubletrack" riding for beginners.

In the first couple of miles, an abandoned dirt road goes through pastures and an occasional herd of cattle — be sure to close the gates behind you. The grade is either level or goes up and down slightly. There is one major stream crossing. At the beginning of the trail, you'll ride through several large meadows until the terrain turns into a mostly forested area.

At 2.5 is the turnoff to Dowdy Lake to your left. The round trip to Dowdy Lake from this point in the trail is 2.4 miles. You can do this now or on the way back from Mt. Margaret. Dowdy is one of the many Red Feather Lakes that this area of the state is known for. The lake has some nice sandy beaches, which makes it a great place to stick your feet in or even go swimming in if it's warm enough. If you don't go to the lake, your roundtrip mileage to Mt. Margaret will be about 7 miles.

At 3.2, you will come to another junction in a clearing. One trail goes more or less straight ahead and is fairly level, while the other one goes downhill and to the right. Don't take that one; go straight. The trail soon turns into interesting singletrack that weaves between rocks and trees, dips, and goes up and down a few small hills. At 3.5, you reach a sign that reads "Mt. Margaret." Behind the sign is what appears to be a pile of rocks about 30 feet high.

Take the 30-second hike to the top of the pile and you'll be much more impressed: sweeping views of several peaks, rock formations and valley floor in front of you. The elevation of Mt. Margaret (7,957 ft.) is actually lower than the trailhead (8,040) you started from.

On the way back, the side road to Dowdy Lake is a gradual climb, so the ride back to the main trail will be a glide. Speaking of the main trail, stay on it. Besides the Dowdy Lake trail, there are other trails and abandoned roads crossing the main trail. Take mental notes of where you've been.

WHILE YOU'RE THERE

Living in the Denver area, I had a tendency to keep my blinders on when it came to traveling to the mountains: I would almost always go west on I-70 or southwest from Denver to the Buena Vista/Salida area. And after looking at the map, I thought the Red Feather Lakes area looked like a major trek from Denver — at least three hours one way. What I discovered was that this is an extremely attractive, off-the-beaten path mountainous area with small communities, little development and plenty of camping, hiking and biking opportunities. The area reminds me more of the Adirondack Mountain villages in Upstate New York than Colorado. There are several small lakes, campgrounds and rustic cabins. And one big surprise: I reached the Mt. Margaret trailhead in exactly two hours, so it's an easy day trip.

For more information on this area, see: **Red Feather District Ranger** *listing in the Recreational Resources in the back of this book.*

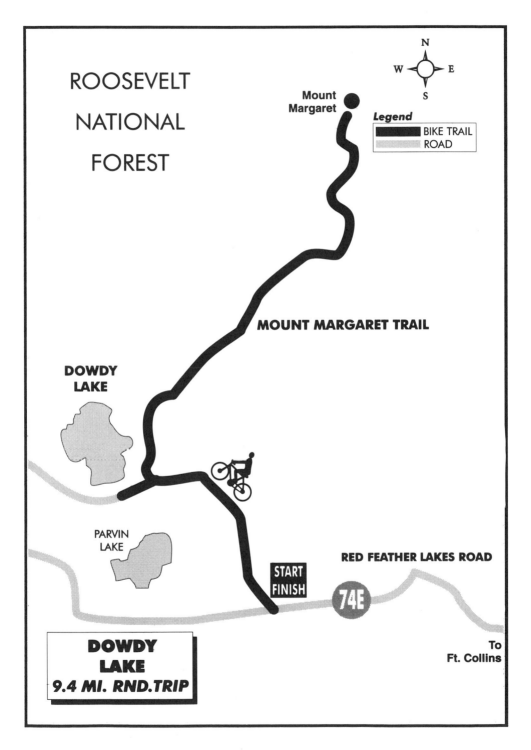

ROOSEVELT
NATIONAL
FOREST

Mount Margaret

N
W E
S

Legend
BIKE TRAIL
ROAD

MOUNT MARGARET TRAIL

DOWDY
LAKE

PARVIN
LAKE

START
FINISH

RED FEATHER LAKES ROAD

74E

To
Ft. Collins

DOWDY
LAKE
9.4 MI. RND.TRIP

O'HAVER LAKE, MARSHALL PASS

You can get a bird's eye view of O'Haver Lake (above) by taking a short ride on the Marshall Pass road, a gentle railroad grade. You can follow the road to the top of Marshall Pass and get views similar to those in the photo below.

O'HAVER LAKE

DISTANCE: 7 miles — loop
ABILITY LEVEL: Easy I
Suitable for children
TRAIL TYPE: 80% dirt road; 20% singletrack
CLIMBS: Gradual climb to lake; downhill return
ELEVATION RANGE: 9,000-9,300 ft.
MAPS: USFS: San Isabel National Forest;
USGS: Poncha Pass, Mt. Ouray (BOTH)
DRIVING TIME FROM DENVER: 3 hours

Get an aerial view of a mountain lake

This is a nice easy ride for the beginner who wants to ride a smooth surface with a gentle grade and get both bird's eye and closeup views of a beautiful little mountain lake.

GETTING THERE
Take U.S. 285 south out of Denver through Fairplay and the town of Poncha Springs. Continue south for six miles until Forest Service Road 243; turn right. (There will be signs for Marshall Pass.) Drive west on FS Road 243 for two miles. Turn right onto the O'Haver Lake Road. Follow this road for one mile — to the Marshall Pass turnoff on the right and park here.

ON THE TRAIL
Start riding on the Marshall Pass Road toward Marshall Pass, which is 12 miles away. Don't worry, you won't go that far — if you don't want to. The entire ride is on a relatively smooth road, which follows an old railroad bed. The grade is never more than 2 percent. However, most of the O'Haver Lake ride is between 9,000 and 9,300 feet above sea level. Marshall Pass and the Continental Divide are at 10,842 feet.

At about 1.5, you'll begin seeing a mountain range to the right. At 2.5, you'll get a bird's eye view of O'Haver Lake, which you will soon be riding toward. Right after you pass O'Haver Lake, start looking to the left, down a short embankment. You will see a metal sign that reads: "No motorized vehicles beyond this point." Walk your bike down the embankment and start riding on this relatively smooth singletrack trail. (There is a sign just past the beginning of this trail on the Marshall Pass Road for Gray's Creek; if you reach it, you have gone too far.)

The trail parallels Gray's Creek, which you can hear or see for most of the ride. The trail soon turns into a narrow little-used dirt road that takes you to the back side of the O'Haver Lake campground. Follow the campground road around to the O'Haver Lake access road, which will bring you back down to your car.

WHILE YOU'RE THERE

Check out the O'Haver Lake campground; it's got one the nicest mountain-lake settings for a campground (although it is actually a small reservoir). The setting makes it extremely popular, so plan to come early or at off-peak times to get a camping spot. Even if you don't camp here, the fishing is rumored to be decent and it's a great place for a picnic.

If you're feeling energetic after this ride, you may want to ride to the Continental Divide on the Marshall Pass Road you were just on. The grade is very gentle and the road is well-maintained. It is 12 miles to the Divide. If you're not feeling *that* energetic, you can always drive to the top to enjoy the view — the road is usually suitable for two-wheel drive cars.

You also might do some exploring in either a four-wheel drive or two-wheel drive vehicle on many of the old mining roads in the area.

For information on this area, see: **Buena Vista, Upper Arkansas Valley** *listings in the Recreational Resources section in the back of this book.*

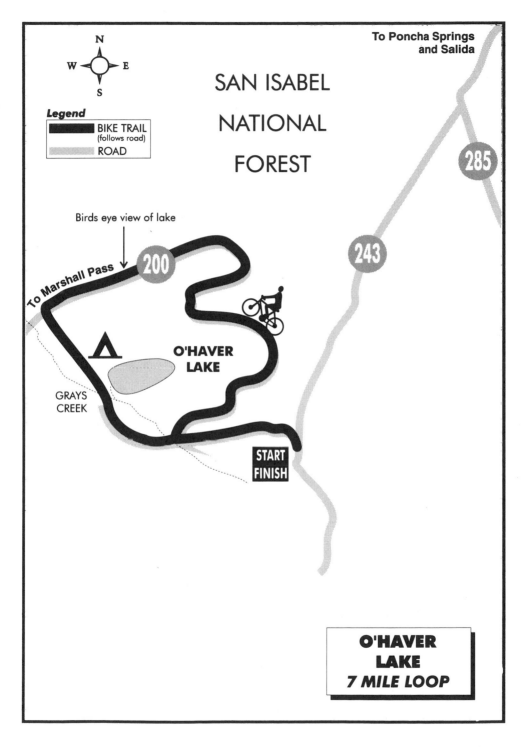

To Poncha Springs
and Salida

SAN ISABEL
NATIONAL
FOREST

Legend
BIKE TRAIL
(follows road)
ROAD

Birds eye view of lake

To Marshall Pass

200

243

285

O'HAVER
LAKE

GRAYS
CREEK

START
FINISH

O'HAVER
LAKE
7 MILE LOOP

RAMPART RESERVOIR

Unusual rock formations (right) can be seen in and around Rampart Reservoir. It is a glistening showcase for Pikes Peak, which looms above this beautiful body of water (below).

RAMPART RESERVOIR

DISTANCE:	11.9 miles — loop
ABILITY LEVEL:	Moderate I
TRAIL TYPE:	90% singletrack; 10% paved road
CLIMBS:	Several short hills; no sustained climbs
ELEVATION RANGE:	9,000-9,220 ft.
MAPS:	USGS: Cascade, CO; USFS: Pike National Forest; Trails Illustrated: No. 137, Pikes Peak
DRIVING TIME FROM DENVER:	1.5 hours

Take a loop around a lofty lake

This wonderful singletrack trail takes you completely around Rampart Reservoir, a beautiful body of water with dozens of curving beaches, unusual rock formations and tree-lined shores. While parts of the trail are a little tricky, a Moderate I rider should be able to handle it.

GETTING THERE

From Denver, drive south on I-25 to Colorado Springs and take the exit for U.S. 24 west. Drive to Woodland Park and turn right onto the Rampart Range Road at the McDonald's. Follow the signs for Rampart Reservoir and Rampart Recreation Area until you get to the parking lot (about 13 miles from U.S. 24) directly on the reservoir dam. Drive to the far end of the parking lot and look for the paved turnaround, where the trail starts.

ON THE TRAIL

I started the ride from the end of the turnaround in the parking lot on the dam. Many local riders start at the other end of the reservoir using an access trail. (See "While You're There" on next page.) The trail immediately takes a short climb, which enables you to get a great view of some unusual rock formations that frame your lake view in the first .2 of a mile of this ride. All throughout the ride, the trail bends and curves with almost every turn in the lake shore, giving you sweeping views of yet another angle of the lake and Pikes Peak to the southwest.

The first mile or so is semi-technical. You may have to walk your bike through some rocky sections, but there are no sustained climbs on this entire ride.

Be sure to take time to stop and admire the large boulders and other rock formations in and around the water in the first few miles of this ride.

After some mild climbing, the trail levels out between 1.1 and 1.4. Between 1.9 and 2.6, the trail turns "inland" (a couple of hundred yards away from the immediate shoreline) and brings you through a beautiful grove of aspen. Besides tracing the curving lake shore, this trail also "takes a break" from the water several times. One minute, it's large rocks, water and sandy beaches, and the next, an alpine setting of aspen and pine groves. For the beginning rider, there's a technical advantage: The parts of the trail that are away from the shoreline tend to be a lot less rocky and actually very smooth in spots.

For the next couple of miles, there are several small hills that are as much fun as they are work!

At about 7.3, ride away from the lake again and at 7.6, cross a bridge over a creek that feeds the lake. An abandoned dirt access road runs along the creek for about a mile and connects a parking area with the trail.

Most of the remainder of this trail hugs the lake shore as it weaves in and out on its way to the dam. A good portion of this section follows a high ridge along the lake that affords some nice views, but beginners should be careful here. There are some steep banks running along the left side of the trail. It's a long drop-off to the lake; take it easy.

At about 11.5, you'll reach the paved road that will take you to the dam. Take a left onto the pavement and ride another half a mile to reach the parking lot.

WHILE YOU'RE THERE

Rampart Reservoir is another one of those areas where you'll have trouble jamming the numerous outdoor activities into one weekend. There are several campgrounds on and around the lake that connect via trail to the lake trail. Several hiking trails leave from the lake into the surrounding forest. Fishing and boating are also very popular here.

Before crossing the bridge at 7.6, you might want to mosey down the dirt access road that runs along the creek for about a mile and a half. It leads to the Rainbow Gulch Trail parking lot. This is a popular starting point for the lake ride, but it will add almost three miles to your total ride mileage. To reach this parking lot by car, take the same road you drove on to get to the dam but don't go as far. The Raspberry Gulch lot is 4.9 miles from the dam or 8.1 miles from U.S. 24.

For additional information, see: **Pikes Peak Ranger District** *and* **Pikes Peak Country Attractions Association** *in the Recreational Resources section in the back of this book.*

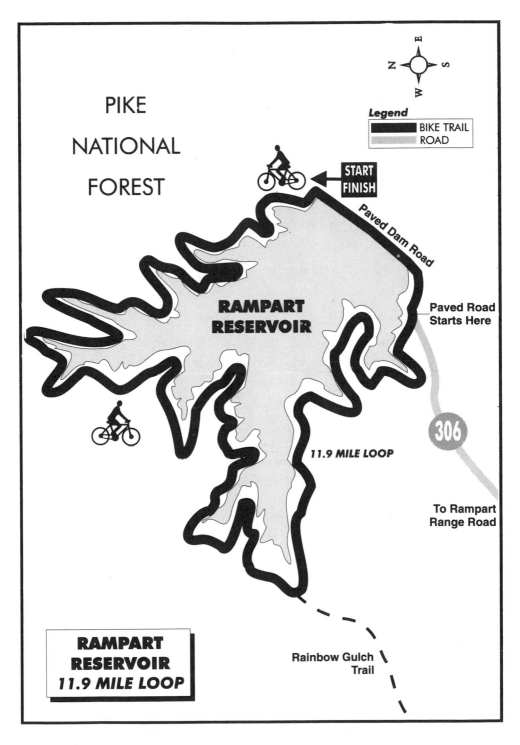

TURQUOISE LAKE

In the first couple miles of the Turquoise Lake trail, you'll be able to peek through the pines and get some spectacular views of the lake and surrounding peaks. Two wilderness areas also surround this beautiful mountain lake.

TURQUOISE LAKE

DISTANCE: 11.5 miles — loop
ABILITY LEVEL: Moderate II
TRAIL TYPE: 50% singletrack; 50% paved road
CLIMBS: Short singletrack climbs; 1.4-mile road climb
ELEVATION RANGE: 9,800-10,200 ft.
MAPS: USFS: San Isabel National Forest;
USGS: Leadville North, Homestake Reservoir
DRIVING TIME FROM DENVER: 2 hours

Wilderness encircles Turquoise Lake

The loop around Turquoise Lake gives the moderate rider a good opportunity to practice some singletrack skills while enjoying views of the lake in a beautiful alpine setting of aspen, pines and wilderness areas that surround the lake. The first half of this ride follows singletrack along the north side of the lake, while most of the second half is on paved road.

GETTING THERE

Drive on I-70 west to the Leadville/U.S. 24 exit. In downtown Leadville, find 6th Street. Turn right, head west, turn right on Turquoise Lake Road and follow this to the boat launching area, where there is plenty of paved parking.

ON THE TRAIL

Start bicycling from the large parking area near the boat launch next to the lake shore. Before taking off, look back toward the reservoir dam to the east. In the distance towers the majestic Mt. Massive, which stands in the designated wilderness area with the same name that surrounds part of the lake. Pick up the singletrack trail along the lake shore from the edge of the parking area, going away from the dam, toward the long part of the lake.

In the first mile or so, the trail is mostly level and smooth as it winds through numerous stands of pine trees and picnic areas. In several spots, the trail peeks out from the pines and puts you right next to the water where you can grab some excellent views of this beautiful lake, Mt. Massive and other 13,000 and 14,000-foot peaks in the distance.

At about 1.0, climb a small ridge that continues to follow the lake shore. At 2.0, ride through a fairly rocky section of trail with boulders on either side followed by a long descent between 2.2 and 2.4. At 2.6, you will have to dismount to get through an extremely rocky section. This section and all others are on either fairly level ground or slight inclines, making walking through them easy. The trail turns away from the lake here and comes back to the lake at 3.5, where you can see the other (west) end of the lake for the first time.

At 4.8, you are sitting on a high ridge overlooking the lake and close enough to see the picnic tables and camping area at the west end. At 5.0, you reach the campground and picnic area — and restrooms! Meander through this paved area for about a mile until you reach the paved road that goes around the lake. Turn left onto this road and start climbing. Most of the remainder of the ride is on pavement.

Climb for 1.4 miles until you reach the top of the hill and the intersection with the Hagerman Pass (dirt) road. You can get a glimpse of the lake from this vantage point. While riding this first section of pavement, you may see backpackers; the Colorado Trail parallels the road to your right here and crosses the stream at the end of the lake.

Cruise through a nice 1.5-mile downhill, climb a little more and glide down to the lake dam.

Immediately (no more than 200 feet) after crossing the dam at 10.8, look for a singletrack trail going off to the left and take it. Follow this little section of roller coaster trail along the lake shore until you get back to your car at the boat launch area.

WHILE YOU'RE THERE

After you've ridden the singletrack portion of this ride at the west end of the lake at 6.0 — before heading back to your car — you might want to check out the *hiking* trail just down the road from the campground here. Instead of turning left onto the paved road from the camping area, turn right, ride .2 of a mile and look for a small clearing/parking area on your left. Ride over to this and look past the stream to the trailhead sign. Follow the trail uphill and across the bridge to reach the sign. This is the trailhead for Timberline Lake in the Holy Cross Wilderness Area, where bikes are prohibited. It's about a three-mile hike one-way to the west. The Colorado Trail also crosses here, and it goes north, also into a designated wilderness area.

Hiking on the Colorado Trail and other trails in the two wilderness areas here is just one of the outdoor activities available at Turquoise Lake. There are several campgrounds on the lake and you'll find many boaters and fishermen in the summer. Warning: The campgrounds fill quickly so try and be the early bird!

*For more information, see: **Leadville** listing in Recreational Resources section in the back of this book.*

VASQUEZ CREEK TRAIL
Returning to Winter Park on the easy Vasquez Creek trail, the bicyclist is treated to some views of the Continental Divide peaks in the distance.

VASQUEZ CREEK

DISTANCE:	9.3 miles — loop
ABILITY LEVEL:	Easy I
	Suitable for children
TRAIL TYPE:	100% relatively smooth, low-traffic dirt road
CLIMBS:	One gradual climb in first 3 miles
ELEVATION RANGE:	8,850-9,200 ft.
MAPS:	USFS: Roosevelt and Arapaho Forests;
	Trails Illustrated: No. 501 Winter Park
DRIVING TIME FROM DENVER:	1.5 hours

An easy Winter Park creekside ride

Do you want a truly easy bike ride that also gives you some great views and the feeling of being in the mountains? This is a great ride for families, beginners and others who want to get out and explore one of the many trails in the Winter Park area. For a little bit of pedaling you get a lot: views of upper and lower Vasquez Creek and the peaks of the Continental Divide.

GETTING THERE:

Drive on I-70 west out of Denver to the Winter Park/U.S. 40 exit. Follow U.S. 40 through Empire (watch for speed traps!), over Berthoud Pass into the town of Winter Park. As you enter the town, look for a two-story retail complex on your left. Turn left here onto Vasquez Road. Drive to the end of this complex and look for the Chamber of Commerce and parking signs. Park here.

ON THE TRAIL

Start in the free parking lot or parking garage (What other bike riding area provides *covered* parking?). Turn right out of the parking lot and head up Vasquez Road and cross the railroad tracks. The pavement soon turns into a well-maintained dirt road, which climbs very gradually along Vasquez Creek. Take a break or two along the creek and enjoy the view to the south, with the mountains of Winter Park Ski Area in the background and the picturesque creek in the foreground.

Between 2 miles and 4 miles, you will see a couple of opportunities to turn left; some of them have trail signs. Keep to the right until you see the sign "Tunnel Hill 152" to your left. As you turn left, you will see a large water diversion dam. Cross the creek here and you're on County Road 152.

With most of the climbing for this ride behind you, watch the Continental Divide unfold in front of you as you ride down the fairly smooth County Road 152. At 7.2, turn left onto the trail marked "Little Vasquez" with a black-and-white sign. Follow this to Arapaho Road and back to the paved Vasquez road to the parking lot.

WHILE YOU'RE THERE

Take a look at the many old logging roads and dedicated mountain biking trails in Winter Park and Fraser. Winter Park is one of the many Colorado winter resort towns that have successfully groomed themselves to lure summer tourists and mountain biking is a big draw here. Where else can you stay in a luxury condo at a discounted summer rate, wake up and pedal to dozens of mountain biking trails directly from the center of town? The routes utilize miles of old logging roads that were carved out of the forest in the early part of this century. For those of you who detest climbing, go to the Winter Park ski resort and put yourself and your mountain bike on the ski lift for a thrilling descent.

For more information on this area, see: **Winter Park/Grand County** *listings in the Recreational Resources section in the back of this book.*

VASQUEZ CREEK
Vasquez Creek gently flows along the Vasquez Creek trail near Winter Park with numerous mountain peaks in the distance.

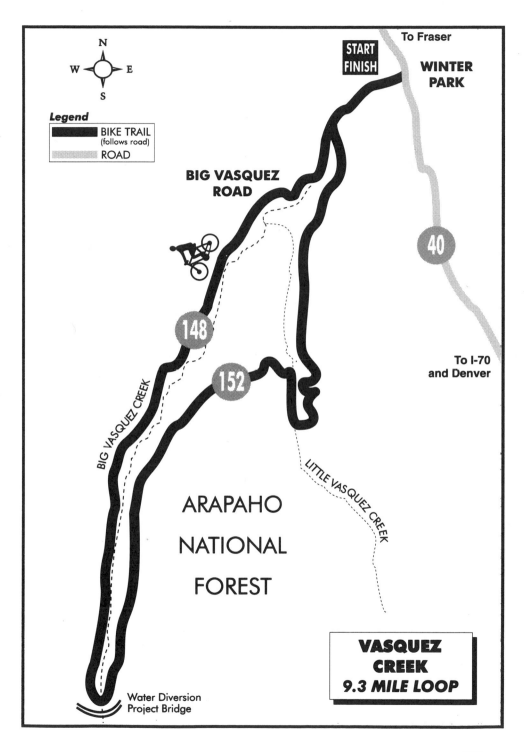

WATERTON CANYON

The Waterton Canyon trail is the most popular easy mountain bike ride in the Denver area because of its gentle grade and proximity to the South Platte River. This trail is the first six miles of the Denver-to-Durango Colorado Trail.

WATERTON CANYON

DISTANCE:	12.4 miles roundtrip
ABILITY LEVEL:	Easy I
	Suitable for children
TRAIL TYPE:	100% wide abandoned dirt road
CLIMBS:	Minimal; few short hills in first half
ELEVATION RANGE:	5,520-5,800 ft.
MAPS:	Map at trailhead or use Colorado Trail map
DRIVING TIME FROM DENVER:	20-30 minutes

Enjoy river on first leg of Colorado Trail

Waterton Canyon is the most popular easy mountain bike ride in the Denver area, as evidenced by the jammed parking lot on weekends. But don't let that scare you. Waterton Canyon is the first 6.2 miles of the Denver-to-Durango Colorado Trail. It is a wonderful place for families, beginners or anyone else who wants to follow Colorado's historic South Platte River. Because this part of the trail is an abandoned road bed, it is a smooth, very wide route to accommodate every bike riding ability. In the many times I have been on the trail, I have never felt it to be crowded, despite the many people on the trail.

GETTING THERE

Drive south on I-25 to the C-470 exit. Drive west on C-470 to the Wadsworth Blvd. exit. Go south (left) on Wadsworth and follow the signs for Chatfield Reservoir and Waterton Canyon. Go past the Chatfield entrance and look for the (marked) road to Waterton to your left. Take this and find the parking lots.

ON THE TRAIL

After squeezing through the unique gate structures (you'll see) at the trailhead, you'll immediately see what you will be seeing for every foot of this trail: the gently flowing water of the South Platte River. The river is what makes the trail users so diverse. You will see entire families riding together (or being pulled in trailers) together, older people out for a leisurely ride by the river, hikers, joggers and a lot of fishermen, mining every turn in the river for their next big catch. A popular fish/ride method here is to carry the fishing rod on the rear rack of the bike. If you've got a rack and rod, give it a shot. On one of my rides, I looked over to the river and saw a hand gingerly holding a string of trout slowly creeping up one of the steep river banks. It was soon followed by a teenage boy.

The grade of the trail is gentle throughout, but you'll be going upstream on the first half of this ride on your way to the Strontia Springs Reservoir. There are a few small climbs, but nothing to huff and puff about. There are also several picnic tables scattered throughout the first few miles of the trail.

The Strontia Springs Reservoir, at 6.2 miles, is the usual terminus for most beginner/intermediate rides. There are places to park your bikes and take a break. Beginners new to dirt road riding should be careful going back. The occasional hill can be very tempting to pick up speed.

WHILE YOU'RE THERE

Instead of turning around at the reservoir, venture up the trail a little more and park (or lock) your bike at the trailhead of the "trail portion" of the Colorado Trail, which brings me to a mini-controversy. Some trail purists claim the "real" Colorado trail doesn't start until this trailhead, because, as you can see, it *looks* like a trail here, not a road. Others say the trail actually begins in the parking lot.

Whoever is right, this part of the *trail* makes a nice hike to top off your bike ride — especially since the remainder of your ride after the hike is mostly a downhill glide. The trail here *does* look like a "real" hiking trail. It carves through dense stands of pine as the canyon narrows and gets even more scenic here. You will see some people biking here, but this is definitely an advanced riding area.

The 469-mile Colorado Trail winds its way through Colorado's central and southwestern mountains on its way to Durango. The existence of the trail is a tribute to thousands of volunteers and several government agencies who worked for more than a dozen years to make the official trail opening a reality on September 4, 1987. Most of the trail is open to mountain biking and the sections in wilderness areas that aren't, have mountain bike alternate routes. You can sample the trail by following the routes in three rides in this book besides this one: Kenosha Pass, Chair Rocks and Buffalo Creek.

For more information on this area, see: **Colorado Tourism Board** *and* **Bicycle Colorado** *listings in the Recreational Resources section in the back of this book.*

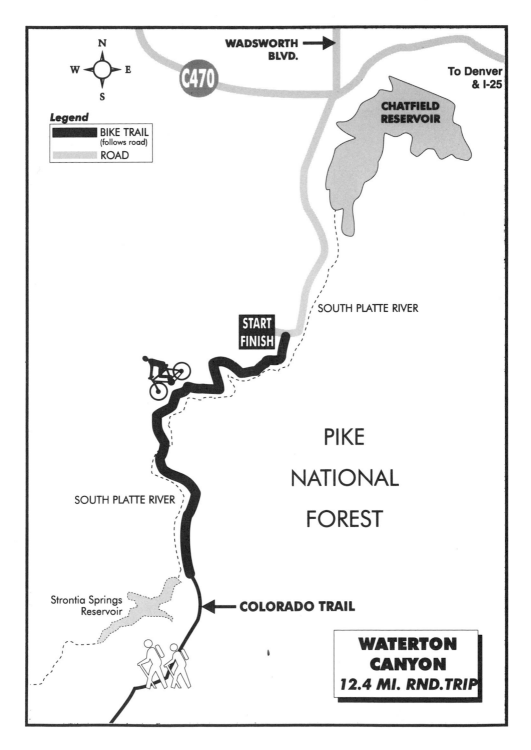

Legend
- BIKE TRAIL (follows road)
- ROAD

WADSWORTH BLVD.

C470

To Denver & I-25

CHATFIELD RESERVOIR

SOUTH PLATTE RIVER

START FINISH

PIKE

NATIONAL

FOREST

SOUTH PLATTE RIVER

Strontia Springs Reservoir

COLORADO TRAIL

WATERTON CANYON
12.4 MI. RND.TRIP

BIKE INTO HISTORY

Colorado and many other parts of the country have been bitten by the bicycle bug. The side effects of this malady are thousands of miles of bicycle paths and routes nationwide.

Residents and government officials alike are finally realizing the benefits of bicycling: more recreation, more fitness, more tourist dollars, better health and less pollution and congestion.

But getting even a 10-mile bike path built for, say, $10 million, is a formidable mountain to climb. And just a *proposal* for a major project, such as a 15-mile bike/recreation path to the Continental Divide, would be laughed at by the official bean counters.

Building roads and railroads through some very unforgiving — but spectacularly scenic — terrain such as mountainsides and the Continental Divide was very serious business for the pioneer miners, road and railroad builders of late 1800s Colorado.

They relied on these first lifelines through the wilderness to haul out precious ores and bring in vital supplies and passengers. Some of the railroads even did a healthy tourist business, allowing horse-bound settlers a glimpse at some unforgettable scenery. But as the claims ran dry and the motor vehicle emerged as King of the Road a few decades later, the tracks were torn up and locomotives became scrap metal.

But their legacy remains in the form of hundreds of miles of roads, abandoned railway beds and right-of-ways to places that have become household words to mountain residents and recreational trekkers: Hagerman Pass, Kenosha Pass, Boreas Pass, Chalk Creek, St. Elmo — the list is continuous. Without the back-breaking efforts of the early railroad and road builders, we probably would not have easy access to these wondrous places.

Colorado's settlement process usually followed a pattern. A few wandering miners would discover a gold or silver vein, stake a claim and the word spread quickly. Hundreds of others would stake claims. A handful would strike it rich. The rest would work for them and help settle a town or community.

After the initial excitement died down, they faced the harsh reality of hauling millions of tons of rock (ore) out of some treacherous places that were difficult to even *walk* to. The horse-drawn wagon was painfully slow and its capacity was limited, although most of the first routes to the mining camps were primitive roads.

Railroads were the key to converting their rock into riches and transforming holes in the ground into thriving communities. Still, building railroads was an expensive and often risky undertaking. What happened if the mines ran out? Will tourist business be enough to keep the railroad financially afloat? Could we keep the rails clear during the long and harsh Colorado winters? Railroad companies were sold often and receiverships and bankruptcies were common.

Because government financial assistance was virtually non-existent at that time, most railroads were privately financed by the railroad companies or even the mining companies.

One of the ways early railroaders cut costs was to build "narrow gauge" lines. A narrow gauge railway measures 3 feet between rails, compared to the much wider standard gauge, which had a space of 4-feet-8-inches between rails. The narrow gauge was cheaper to build and also adapted much better to the many curves and switchbacks of the mountain routes they had to negotiate.

Today, only a few narrow gauge lines still operate, and the majority of these are for tourists. But the railway beds the builders left behind are used year-round by mountain bikers, hikers, four-wheel-drive vehicles, skiers and snowmobilers.

Many of the rides in this book are on railway beds originally built in the 1800s. Following are brief accounts of the history of the mountain bike routes in this section of the book.

Boreas Pass

The riches of Colorado's gold and silver mines were the magnet that drew the Denver, South Park & Pacific Railroad through 340 miles of rugged terrain in Colorado's mountains.

The railroad began serving the little mining settlement of Boreas atop the Continental Divide and the bustling town of Breckenridge in 1882.

Breckenridge was born in 1859 in the same way many other mountain towns were at that time: with a major gold strike. Word of the strike spread and the population of the town ballooned, until it was about 8,000 in the late 1800s.

Most of the gold mines were played out by the early 1900s and the railroad was abandoned in the late 1930s because of a lack of ridership, the burgeoning automobile and the economic repercussions of the Depression.

In its heyday in the late 1800s, Boreas boasted a post office, a telegraph office, and a stone engine house. Today, only portions of the log post office building remain.

Midland Bicycle Trail

A dedicated bicycle trail traces about five miles of the Colorado Midland Railroad, which served more than 50 Colorado communities from Colorado Springs to Glenwood Springs along its 261-mile route in the late 1800s and early 1900s.

Mining was also the reason for the development of this rail line, but many of the communities on its route actually owe their founding and growth to the railroad's existence. The smaller communities it served included Woodland Park, Hartsel and Spinney, while its prominent stops were Aspen, Leadville and Glenwood Springs.

Although the Midland was one of Colorado's longest-lived narrow gauge railroads, it succumbed to federal bureaucracy, insolvency and a lack of ridership and was abandoned in 1921.

The New Santa Fe Trail

The New Santa Fe Trail, a 15-mile hiking and biking path starting in Palmer Lake, sits on the abandoned railway bed of General William Palmer's Denver & Rio Grande Railway, which was chartered in 1870.

While most railroads starting up in Colorado at that time were lured to the west by the state's growing mineral deposits, the D&RG was the only railroad to orient itself north and south instead of east-west.

In fact, Palmer and his railroad were responsible for the founding and development of many southern Colorado towns and cities in the 1870s, including Colorado Springs, Pueblo and Palmer Lake.

Palmer Lake was an important stop for the D&RG. After steadily "puffing" up the incline from the east to reach the small lakeside town, the locomotives' water supplies were exhausted and they used the lake as a refueling stop. The railroad also carried thousands of tourists to Palmer Lake on the weekends.

While hauling gold and silver ores was important to the new railroad, Palmer spotted another market from the inception of the railroad: coal. Colorado's growing population and mining industries needed coal to prosper. The Denver & Rio Grande carried millions of tons of coal out of the southern Colorado mines.

After "conquering" southern Colorado, Palmer had big plans of extending his narrow gauge railroad to Mexico. But financial problems, including taking on debt to modernize the railroad and the Panic of 1873, hit the railroad hard and expansion plans were scrapped. It maneuvered many stormy financial seas in the early 1900s and most of the narrow gauge track had been abandoned by the early 1940s.

St. Elmo

St. Elmo was a classic mining community of the late 1800s. It boomed for a couple decades and a sizable community was built. But when its main gold source, The Mary Murphy Mine, was played out in the early 1900s, the town quickly declined and the railroad soon followed.

In its heyday, the town had many businesses, including five hotels and a newspaper. St. Elmo was a hub for the Denver, South Park & Pacific Railroad, the same line that served Breckenridge and Boreas. Passengers would board the train for Denver to the east and the other mining towns of Aspen to the north and Tincup to the west.

The town was also a party and supply town for the hundreds of miners that lived in and around the town. The town population got as high as about 1,500.

Today, St. Elmo is a living ghost town. Many of the old buildings are privately owned and occupied. It is a favorite spot for summer tourists and four-wheel drive vehicles heading up to Tincup and Gunnison County.

Waldorf Mine

Minister and mining entrepreneur John Wilcox needed an economical way to get the ore from his 65 mining properties in the high valley and hillsides above Georgetown to the mill and market. The mines were booming, but the horse and wagon was slow and unreliable on the steep mountain road.

Once he got the ore down to Silver Plume near Georgetown, he could ship it on the Colorado Central Railroad that served Georgetown from Denver.

In August 1905, Wilcox began building the Argentine Central Railroad Railway to serve his mines in the "Argentine" mining district above Georgetown. The Argentine name was apparently derived from Argentum, the Latin name for silver ore.

Exactly one year later, the train began running on the 15.9-mile route from Silver Plume to the top of McClellan Mountain (13,587 feet). In the same month that the railroad began serving the mines in the area, it carried hundreds of tourists to the top of McClellan Mountain, which is near the "fourteeners," Grays Peak and Torreys Peak.

One major stop was the mining community of Waldorf, which was where most of Wilcox's mines were located. The small settlement sat in a beautiful high-mountain valley surrounded by 13,000 and 14,000-foot peaks.

But tourism and mining could not justify the investment of more than $200,000 that was made in the railroad. After the silver market and economy declined and America became involved in World War I, the Argentine Central was abandoned in 1918, just 13 years after it was born.

Today, The Argentine Central Railway route is a favorite of mountain bikers, "four-wheelers" and hikers on Grays and Torreys Peaks.

BOREAS PASS

Parts of the post office and train depot log buildings are all that's standing atop of Boreas Pass on the Continental Divide, but there's plenty of natural beauty to see at the Divide and on the way there. Below is the Goose Pasture Tarn (a small mountain lake) in the foreground, with Fletcher Mountain and Pacific Peak looming overhead.

BOREAS PASS

DISTANCE: 12.4 miles roundtrip
ABILITY RATING: Easy II
TRAIL TYPE: Dirt road the entire route
CLIMBS: Continuous gradual climb 1st half
ELEVATION RANGE: 10,360-11,481 ft.
MAPS: Trails Illustrated: No. 109, Breckenridge;
USFS: Arapaho National Forest
DRIVING TIME FROM DENVER: 1.5 hours

Bike to the Continental Divide with ease

This is one of the more popular rides in the Breckenridge area for good reason. Despite the climbing, beginners can handle it with relative ease. Riders of all abilities get a decent workout and everybody gets some great mountain views on the way up. At the top, they can say: "I *biked* to the Continental Divide!"

GETTING THERE

On the south end of the town of Breckenridge, turn left onto the Boreas Pass Road. Drive past the condos and expensive homes overlooking the ski area and valley for about 3.5 miles. Park in the parking area just before the paved road turns into a dirt road.

ON THE TRAIL

The first half of this ride, on the way to Boreas Pass and the Continental Divide, is all climbing. But thanks to builders of the Denver, South Park and Pacific Railroad in the late 1800s, the grade is never very steep and most of the route is only mildly rocky. But that doesn't mean you won't work for it. The altitude of this ride, ranging from 10,360 feet to 11,481 feet, combined with steady climbing on a dirt road, may cause more than a few riders to stop and catch their breath.

The good news is, while you're taking in some extra oxygen, there's literally dozens of places to stop and take in the fantastic scenery. Shortly after leaving the parking area at the beginning of the dirt portion of the road, start noticing a small lake below you to the right surrounded by peaks. That's the Goose Pasture Tarn (a tarn is a small mountain lake), which is at the confluence of the Blue River and Indiana Creek. Beyond the water are four peaks (left to right): Mt. Helen, Pacific Peak, Crystal Peak and Peak 10. The Blue River runs through this entire valley. You'll also get a glimpse of the ski trails carved out by the Breckenridge ski area.

In the first three miles of this ride, many sections of the road are draped with canopies of aspen tree branches — great "photo ops" in the fall. The photo on the front cover of this book was taken on this part of the Boreas Pass Road.

At 3.0, you'll reach Baker's Tank, a critical water refueling tank for the narrow gauge railroad engines that once toiled up this incline. The 9,305-gallon tank is more than 100 years old.

Continue on the remainder of the 6.2 miles to Boreas Pass and the Continental Divide. Watch the terrain change as you begin to rise above timberline: from aspen and pine groves to low-lying brush and rocky terrain. In mid-summer, you may even see patches of wildflowers.

Boreas Pass is a great place for a break or lunch. Take in the natural and man-made sites. Still standing are portions of the train depot and post office buildings that were once part of the thriving Boreas settlement on the top of the pass. Boreas' claim to fame was the highest post office building in the U.S. and the only post office building to straddle the Continental Divide. (Read more about the history of Boreas in the beginning of this section.)

Explore the rolling meadows and foot trails here and enjoy the panoramic view of the vast South Park and the Ten Mile Range to the west.

Enjoy the cruise back down, but watch your speed! You may catch a rock or rut.

WHILE YOU'RE THERE

If you can arrange it, drop a car off in Como, on the other end of the Boreas Pass Road. The 11 miles from Boreas Pass to Como is not that tough, but I would definitely not recommend it unless you're car shuttling — it's a long climb back!

The first three miles of the Boreas Pass road to Baker's Tank is also a popular cross-country skiing area in the winter because of its relatively gentle grade and panoramic views. Breckenridge bustles with skiers in the winter, but it is also a fun mountain town in the summer and fall. Breckenridge hosts several music festivals in the summer and has recently started an annual film festival in late September.

For more information on this area, see: **Summit County** *listings in the Recreational Resources section in the back of this book.*

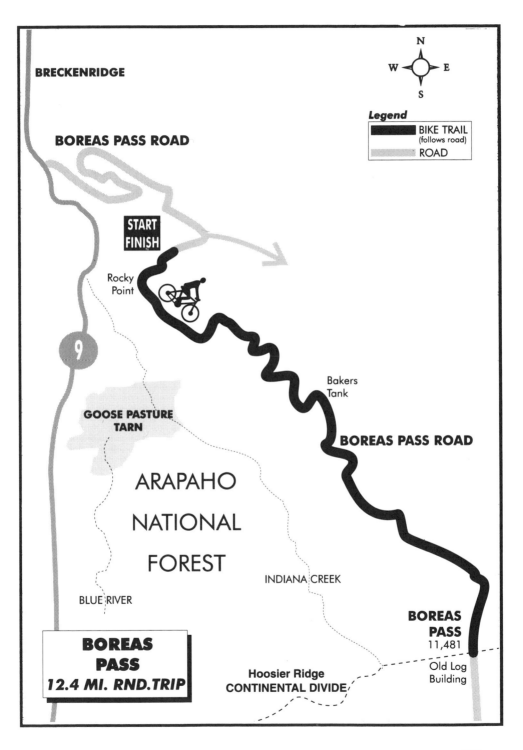

MIDLAND BIKE TRAIL

The Midland Bike Trail (above) follows the abandoned railroad grade of the Midland Railroad, which stopped running in the early 1920s. To start the trail, bicyclists must cross the Arkansas River (below) on a foot bridge.

MIDLAND BIKE TRAIL

DISTANCE:	16 miles roundtrip
ABILITY LEVEL:	Moderate II
TRAIL TYPE:	75% singletrack; 25% dirt road
CLIMBS:	Toughest climb first mile out of river canyon
ELEVATION RANGE:	8,000-8,700 ft.
MAPS:	USFS: San Isabel;
	Trails Illustrated: No. 129, Buena Vista
DRIVING TIME FROM DENVER:	2.25 hours

Peek into the past, get view of valley

The Midland Bike Trail is a dedicated bike route that follows the abandoned bed of the Colorado Midland Railroad. Although the railroad served more than 50 communities between Colorado Springs and Glenwood Springs, it was abandoned in 1922. Only the actual rails were taken up: You will see many of the original railroad ties still lying (and decaying) where they were left. The route features outstanding views of the Upper Arkansas Valley and the mountain peaks surrounding it, the Arkansas River and the harsh beauty of the terrain that the pioneers had to carve a railroad bed through. (Read more about the history of the "Midland" at the beginning of this section.)

GETTING THERE
From Denver, take U.S. 285 south through Fairplay to U.S. 24 and go north (right) into Buena Vista. Near the center of town turn east (right) onto Main Street and follow this past a ball park on the left to a riverside park. Park here and look for a foot bridge across the Arkansas River, where you will start pedaling.

ON THE TRAIL
You can start biking at either end of the Midland Trail, either here or at the Shields Gulch trailhead on the other end. I chose to start at the "low" end — elevation wise — so that the ride back would be pretty much of a cruise.

After crossing the Arkansas River, follow the trail to the right and don't go up the trail with steps to your left. Go past the steps and continue along the river. At about .4, it will start winding up the river canyon to the left and eventually intersect with a dirt road, County Road 304, at about 1.1. Turn right onto the road and follow this for another 2.5 miles until you reach the Midland Bike Trail trailhead sign. On the way to the trailhead, enjoy the views of the Arkansas River and the Upper Arkansas Valley below and the majestic Sawatch Range and Collegiate Peaks of

Mt. Princeton, Mt. Harvard and Mt. Yale in the background. The Arkansas River starts its journey across four states less than 50 miles up this valley near Leadville.

The first mile of the actual trail (3.6-4.6) has some short, steep climbs that take you through, up and down some gullies, but nothing that can't be handled by the experienced beginner or moderate rider. The trail surface is moderately rocky in places. After about a mile of this, you'll glide through some relatively flat stretches accompanied by some "mini" canyons: small rock formations on both sides of the trail that you will bike through. (Imagine squeezing a railroad locomotive through some of these areas!)

In the next mile or so (4.6-5.5), you will encounter a few more short, steep hills to go up and down. After these climbs, take a break and look to the direction you came from and you'll see the beautiful Collegiate Peaks continue to unfold.

You'll be able to take a longer look on your way back, as you will be riding toward them. In the last couple of miles of this ride, you'll see more decaying railroad ties along the trail, as you ascend a couple more short hills. In the final mile or so, you'll have an easy ride to the Shields Gulch trailhead. If you are returning immediately, you might stop at the last hill overlooking the Shields Gulch trailhead (you'll see the back side of the big brown trailhead sign) and turn around there; there are no facilities at the trailhead.

WHILE YOU'RE THERE

The dedicated bike trail ends at the Shields Gulch trailhead, but there is plenty of good bike riding beyond this trailhead on the two-wheel drive and four-wheel drive dirt roads that honeycomb this large U.S. Forest Service region. Explore by car first and see what you like.

Mountain biking is just one of the many outdoor activities to keep you busy in the Upper Arkansas Valley. Hiking the "fourteeners" in the nearby Collegiate Peaks near Buena Vista and rafting the rapids of the Arkansas have exploded in recent years. When I lived in Salida in the late 1970s as a newspaper reporter, the two fledgling rafting companies begged me to go on a "press excursion" to publicize the fledgling venture. (I obliged.) Today, there are dozens of rafting companies up and down the Arkansas competing for your business. Despite the popularity of this area, it has managed to stay "small townish" and relatively condo-free, unlike the popular ski resort towns. Like other mountain communities, they have discovered the popularity of mountain biking in the Upper Arkansas Valley. There are many bike shops to buy and rent from, both in Buena Vista and Salida.

For more information on this area, see: ***Buena Vista, Upper Arkansas Valley*** *listings in the Recreational Resources section of this book.*

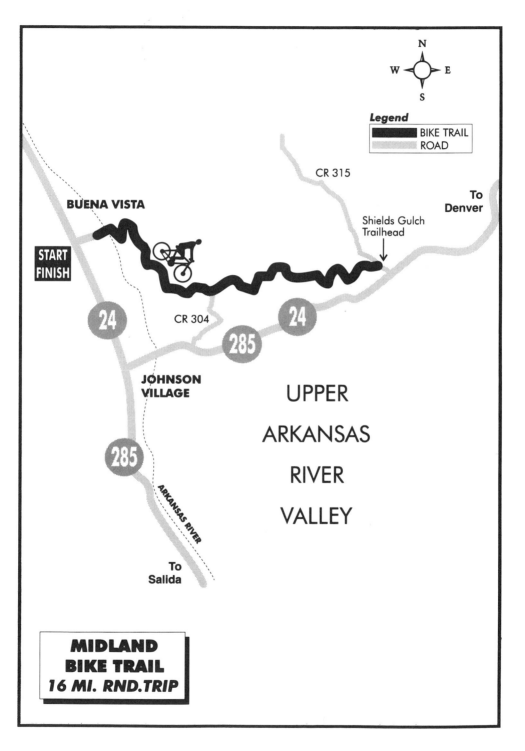

Legend
BIKE TRAIL
ROAD

CR 315

To Denver

BUENA VISTA

Shields Gulch Trailhead

START FINISH

24

CR 304

285

24

JOHNSON VILLAGE

UPPER

ARKANSAS

RIVER

VALLEY

285

ARKANSAS RIVER

To Salida

MIDLAND BIKE TRAIL 16 MI. RND. TRIP

NEW SANTA FE TRAIL
This pastoral scene greets bicyclists in the second half of the New Santa Fe Trail on the grounds of the
U.S. Air Force Academy.

NEW SANTA FE TRAIL

DISTANCE:	30 miles roundtrip; shorter options
ABILITY LEVEL:	Easy I
	Suitable for children
TRAIL TYPE:	100% hard-packed (road width) dirt trail
CLIMBS:	Occasional gradual climb; mostly flat
ELEVATION RANGE:	6,300-7,200 ft.
MAPS:	Use maps posted at each trailhead
DRIVING TIME FROM DENVER:	1 hour

Ride a railroad bed into history

Beginning riders, children and other mountain bikers who just want to go for a cruise will enjoy this ride. While the length of this ride — 30 miles — is the longest ride in this book, it is also one of the easiest. (You may also take some of the shorter options.) The entire trail is made of a hard-packed sandy surface with absolutely no rocks in sight. In a few places in the second half of the ride, there are a few hills and curves that make it interesting. But otherwise, this bike path follows a very gentle railroad grade through some beautiful foothills scenery northwest of Colorado Springs.

GETTING THERE

Drive on I-25 south toward Colorado Springs, take the Palmer Lake/Larkspur exit and head west to Palmer Lake. As you approach town, you will see a Palmer Lake sign. About .4 of a mile past this sign and right after the "speed limit 30" sign, look for a dirt road to your left and take this. It goes over to the small Palmer Lake. Park at the trailhead/picnic area here. Be sure to read the maps posted at each trailhead.

ON THE TRAIL

At the beginning of the trail itself, there is an interpretive sign explaining the history of the Denver & Rio Grande narrow gauge railroad; this trail is on its abandoned railroad bed. (See the introduction to this section for the history of the railroad.) From the very beginning of the trail, there are panoramic views of the green valley floor meeting the foothills to the west. A modern-day working train parallels the bike trail in many spots. It's just close enough for children to see and hear a "REAL train!" but far enough way for safety.

Follow the level, lightly sandy trail to another park at 3.5, the Monument trailhead. Here, you'll encounter your first climb of any size, and it isn't much. At 6.0, the trail begins to climb and twist a little more compared to what you've already ridden on, but it's still very easy riding.

At about this point, the trail starts to parallel Interstate 25 for a short distance. Just after 9.0, you'll enter the U.S. Air Force Academy grounds. Don't worry, there are no checkpoints or changing of the guard, but children will get a glimpse of a military plane on display at the Academy entrance. You can see the auto entrance (and the aircraft) from a bridge here. To get a closer look, you can bicycle the short spur trail that goes off to the right down to the entrance.

Just after entering the Academy grounds, the trail starts descending into a more heavily forested area — the type of terrain you have been viewing from afar until this point. One of the interpretive signs along the trail explains this change in the terrain. "The confluence of prairie, foothill and riparian (river or stream bank habitat) communities along the Front Range create Colorado's richest habitat for wildlife." Follow a low, more densely vegetated area for the next few miles.

Toward the end of the ride (at 14.2), you could legitimately imagine that you've been transported more than 200 miles to southwestern Colorado. Off to the left of the trail, there is a miniature cave along Monument Creek, in the same color stone as the full-sized ancient Indian cave dwellings found in southwestern Colorado and northern New Mexico.

At 15.0, you'll get to another small park and parking lot, the Ice Lake trailhead. You can turn around here or go another .5 of a mile further, where the trail dead-ends at the Academy grounds boundary.

SHORTER OPTIONS

If you've ridden 30 miles on a bicycle on pavement, you'll have no problem with this ride. However, you or younger riders with you may want to use the accompanying map to pick a good spot to turn around or use a car shuttle to ride the entire length. Here are the distances of the various trailheads/parks from Palmer Lake: Monument: 3.5 miles; Baptist Road: 6.5; North Gate Road: 9.4; Ice Lake trailhead:15.0. Double these distances if you're starting and ending at Palmer Lake.

WHILE YOU'RE THERE

Although Palmer Lake itself does not match the grandeur of other mountain lakes, it is nestled in a quaint foothills community of cabins and a few shops. There are several spots along the lake shore to enjoy a picnic. On the north side of the lake, there's a fenced-in narrow gauge railroad locomotive on display. You aren't the only one yearning for a Sunday outing in this area. At the beginning of this century, "wildflower excursions" were sponsored by the Denver & Rio Grande Railroad and brought many people to the Columbine Park area near the lake to pick flowers. The 115-mile trip from Denver cost $1.00. Since early trains had no dining cars, passengers ate their meals at roadhouses near the depot.

For more information on this area, see: **Pikes Peak Country Attractions Association** *in the Recreational Resources section in the back of this book.*

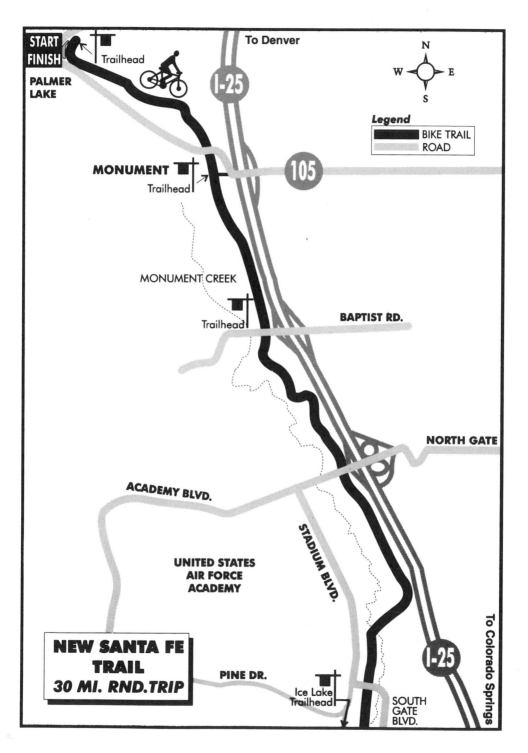

START FINISH

Trailhead

PALMER LAKE

To Denver

I-25

N
W · E
S

Legend
BIKE TRAIL
ROAD

MONUMENT
Trailhead

105

MONUMENT CREEK

Trailhead

BAPTIST RD.

NORTH GATE

ACADEMY BLVD.

STADIUM BLVD.

UNITED STATES
AIR FORCE
ACADEMY

NEW SANTA FE TRAIL
30 MI. RND.TRIP

PINE DR.

Ice Lake
Trailhead

SOUTH
GATE
BLVD.

I-25

To Colorado Springs

ST. ELMO

Cyclists on this ride will see the still-living "ghost town" of St. Elmo (below) and Cascade Falls in Chalk Creek (right.).

ST. ELMO

DISTANCE: 14.6 miles — loop
ABILITY LEVEL: Moderate I
TRAIL TYPE: 100% dirt road
CLIMBS: One tough climb just after Alpine Lake
ELEVATION RANGE: 9,000-9,900 ft.
MAPS: USFS: San Isabel;
Trails Illustrated: No. 130, St. Elmo
DRIVING TIME FROM DENVER: 2.5 hours

Bike to a living ghost town

This ride is good for the bicyclist who is ready for a longer ride on a slightly rough surface, but not rocky singletrack — yet. This ride takes you past some wonderful cascades in Chalk Creek, a private mountain lake and the historic mining town of St. Elmo, where the buildings are still occupied by private owners.

GETTING THERE

Take U.S. 285 south through Fairplay and Johnson Village to the junction of CR 162 south of Buena Vista and follow the signs for Mt. Princeton Hot Springs. Drive on 162 for approximately 10 miles (along Chalk Creek) and look for the signs for Cascade Falls and Cascade Campground. In this area, you will see a large trailhead parking area for "Agnes Vaille Falls" on the right. Park here. You can also park in the "Angler Parking" area on the left side of the road and Cascade Falls parking area on the right; they're all within about a mile of each other.

ON THE TRAIL

Turn right out of the parking area and start biking on the dirt County Road 162 along Chalk Creek. At about 1.0 mile, you will start seeing Cascade Falls. Stop in the little parking area, take a few pictures of the creek cascading over several hundred feet and continue up the road. About 1.5 miles from where you started is the turnoff for County Road 292. Turn right here.

Shortly after turning onto 292 (2.0), you'll see beaver ponds on the left. While this is a maintained dirt road, it seems more like an alpine trail at times. Beautiful groves of aspen crowd both sides of the road in many places, creating an aspen tunnel to ride through. The road winds and climbs gently until it drops you down to Alpine Lake at about 4.0.

Take the road that forks to the right and start riding around Alpine Lake. You can take some nice pictures of the lake and mountains in the background, but please don't leave the road right-of-way; this is private property.

The town of Alpine was a booming community in this area in the late 1800s, when the railroad ended here. For a short time, the town had more than 500 residents, three banks, a smelter, two hotels and more than 20 saloons! But when the railroad extended to St. Elmo and made that town a hub, most of the residents moved and took their buildings with them! Today, only a few scattered cabins remain.

After your lake break, start heading up the road. This is probably the toughest climb on this ride. CR 292 climbs for about a half a mile and it is rocky in places. Go ahead and walk it — no one's looking! The road levels off, then climbs a little more until you reach Iron City, once the site of a smelter and power plant.

Just past Iron City, you will reach the still-living town of St. Elmo. Many of the original buildings of this once-bustling gold mining town are not only still standing, but still occupied; they are all privately owned. (Read more about the town's history at the beginning of this section.) This is an excellent place to take a lunch break. You can picnic in the small town park near Chalk Creek and ride around on the dirt roads. After lunch, you're ready to take a mostly downhill cruise to your car. You will be riding for about 7 miles on County Road 162. This road can get fairly steady traffic in the peak summer months, but the drivers are courteous.

WHILE YOU'RE THERE

This is a wonderful area to camp, bike, explore and take a dip in the hot springs! In the area along County Road 162 where you parked, there are three camping areas: Mt. Princeton, Chalk Lake and Cascade Campgrounds. You can hike the trail to Agnes Vaille Falls or sample the Colorado Trail, which intersects County Road 162 about three miles before you reach the parking area at Agnes Vaille Falls trailhead. While mountain bikes are permitted on the Colorado Trail here, beginning riders may want to hike it first; this is more difficult/advanced riding. Four-wheelers can drive past St. Elmo to the old mining town of Tincup. Further down CR 162, toward U.S. 285, don't forget to check out the magnificent Chalk Cliffs — you'll see why they're called that.

After you've done all that, you'll need a dip in the Mount Princeton Hot Springs, which you passed just after you turned onto County Road 162 from U.S. 285. Be sure and try the hot springs as they enter Chalk Creek here — it's a great hot-and-cold sensation!

For more information on this area, see: **Buena Vista Chamber of Commerce, Heart of the Rockies Chamber of Commerce** *and* **San Isabel National Forest** *in the Recreational Resources section in the back of this book.*

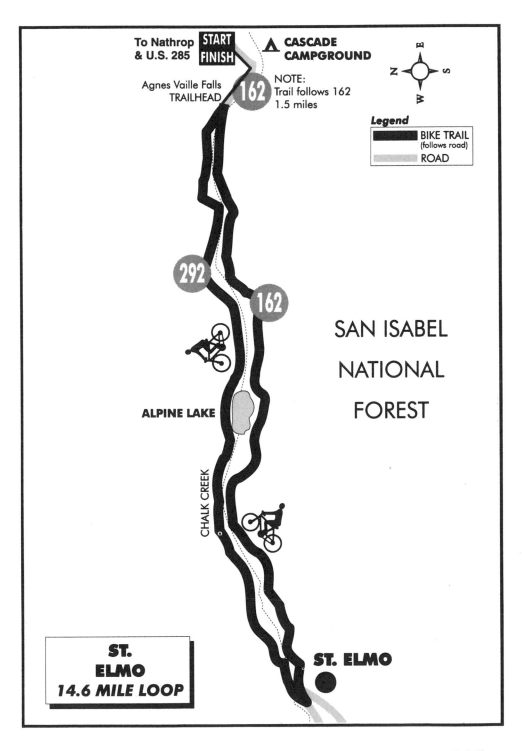

To Nathrop & U.S. 285

START FINISH

Agnes Vaille Falls TRAILHEAD

162

△ **CASCADE CAMPGROUND**

NOTE: Trail follows 162 1.5 miles

292

162

ALPINE LAKE

CHALK CREEK

SAN ISABEL NATIONAL FOREST

ST. ELMO

Legend
BIKE TRAIL (follows road)
ROAD

ST. ELMO 14.6 MILE LOOP

WALDORF MINE

Grays Peak towers above the remains of the
Waldorf Mine settlement above Georgetown. While
no major structures remain, cyclists who venture
up the Waldorf Mine Road (below) are treated to
views of several peaks and a beautiful alpine valley.

WALDORF MINE

DISTANCE:	10 miles roundtrip
ABILITY LEVEL:	Easy II — long climb in 1st half
TRAIL TYPE:	100% 4WD road
CLIMBS:	Most of 1st half continuous climb
ELEVATION RANGE:	10,100-11,594 ft.
MAPS:	USGS 7.5: Georgetown, Grays Peak;
	Trails Illustrated: No. 502, Idaho Springs;
	USFS: Arapaho National Forest
DRIVING TIME FROM DENVER:	1 hour

Visit an old mine, spectacular valley

Forest Service Road 248, the road to the Waldorf Mine, is a good introduction to extended climbing at a high altitude. The views at the end of the climb are stupendous. The climb can be strenuous in spots and climbs to an elevation of 11,594 feet, but it is not a very technical ride. The wide four-wheel drive road gives you plenty of room to dodge any major obstacles. The four-wheel drive traffic is heavier on weekends and other peak times. The road is actually an abandoned railway bed that once carried the Argentine Central Railroad, built by minister-miner John Wilcox in 1906 to serve the Waldorf Mine, the remnants of which you will see at the end of your climb.

GETTING THERE

Head west on I-70 and take the Georgetown exit. Drive through town and look for the blue and white "Scenic Byway" signs for the Guanella Pass Road. Follow this road for 2.5 miles, until it joins with Forest Road 248; you will see a chain link fence. Drive for 1 mile on FS 248, until you come to a large area that is intersected by three roads. Park here.

ON THE TRAIL

After parking your car, take the road that goes up out of the parking area. This fairly steep climb to the next switchback is probably the steepest of your journey.

Continue the long, gradual climb, taking breaks as needed. The road surface varies from very smooth to moderately rocky. This is a good transition for the beginner from smooth dirt road to a moderately rocky surface and steady climbs.

At the beginning of your ride, you'll see a part of the valley behind you, but you are soon swallowed by the large pine trees on either side of the road. You get a glimpse of the peaks ahead of you on your left. At 2.5, a side road goes down to your left; stay on the main road. At 3.5, take a break at the first major vehicle turnaround and enjoy the views of the peaks ahead of you.

While you're resting, go to the side of the road, and peer down the edge to see how much dirt fill and rocks had to be moved in manually by the road and railroad builders in the 1900s to make the grade as "gentle" as it is. Virtually all of this work was done manually. Now the rest of the ride won't feel that bad!

Between 3.5 and 5.0, you'll get progressively better views of the peaks and circs(a circular formation of peaks) above you that will inspire you to pedal a little faster. At 5.0, you get your first reward (the second is the descent!) for your climb: a magnificent high-mountain valley surrounded by circs and several peaks: Grays Peak, Argentine Peak and Mt. Wilcox. On the day I did this ride, in early September, the sky was crystal blue and it had snowed the night before, making the peaks glisten. Poke through the remnants of the Waldorf Mine and the mining settlement of Waldorf: a few piles of lumber that were once a building, a small shed and some tailing piles and ponds.

The town of Waldorf was a once-bustling mining community that included a post office, an "eating house" and boarding house.

After your explorations, head back. For the beginners, you'll notice that the bumps you encounter on the way back seem much more pronounced. That's because — even though you're going fairly slow — you're probably going about 6-8 mph, twice as fast as you came up. Again, this road is a good training ground for more difficult and rocky singletrack.

WHILE YOU'RE THERE

Hikers and more advanced riders may want to continue for two more miles on this railroad bed/road to Argentine Pass or four more miles to the summit of Mt. McClellan, which is near the (hiking) trailhead for Grays Peak. This section is much rockier, and in some sections, steeper than the road to Waldorf.

If you want a little different experience, the company that operates the Georgetown Loop Railroad offers a unique package. They drive you to Waldorf or Mt. McClellan, you bike down and then take a ride on the historic Georgetown Loop narrow gauge railroad to Silver Plume and back. For more information, call the Georgetown Loop Railroad at 303-670-1686.

Either before or after your ride, continue driving up the Guanella Pass Road to Guanella Pass and treat yourself to some great views. There are several trails to hike on (not bike) in this area.

For more information on this area, see: ***Georgetown Chamber of Commerce*** *in the Recreational Resource section in the back of this book.*

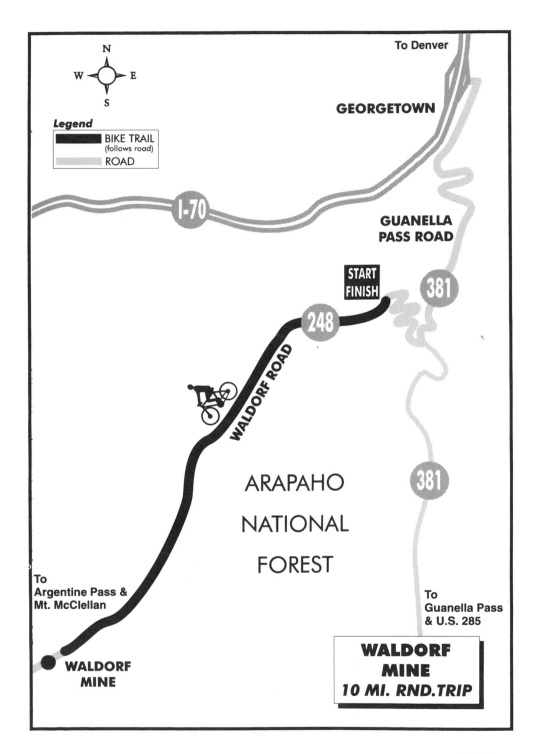

NOTES

Recreational Resources
Who to contact for Colorado bicycling and recreation information

Contact the following agencies for additional information on bicycling, camping, hiking and other forms of recreation in Colorado. For information on specific areas of the state that pertain to the individual rides in this book, refer to the "While You're There" section at the end of each ride; it will tell you which particular agencies in this section to contact for more information.

FOREST SERVICE OFFICES
These offices are excellent sources of information for camping and general recreation information in all U.S. Forest Service areas in the state. Contact either the particular regional office or the Rocky Mountain Regional Office in Golden, which is also where you can purchase maps. In parentheses are the general area of the state each office covers.

U.S. Forest Service Rocky Mountain Regional Office (statewide info.)
740 Simms St., Golden, CO 80401 Visitor information: (303) 275-5350

National Park Service (National Park information)
P.O. Box 25287, Denver, CO 80225 (303) 969-2000

Arapaho, Roosevelt National Forests (Northern Colorado mountains)
240 West Prospect Road, Fort Collins, CO 80526-2098 (303) 498-1100

Boulder District Ranger (Boulder County area)
2995 Baseline Road, Room 110, Boulder, CO 80303 (303) 444-6001

Dillon Ranger District (Dillon Reservoir, Summit County)
135 Highway 9, Blue River Center, P.O. Box 620, Silverthorne, CO 80498 (303) 468-5400

Pikes Peak Ranger District (Pikes Peak, Colo. Springs areas)
601 S. Weber St., Colorado Springs, CO 80903 (719) 636-1602

Red Feather District Ranger (Red Feather Lakes; N. Colorado mountains) 210 E. Olive, Fort Collins, CO 80524 (303) 498-1375

San Isabel National Forest, Forest Supervisor (Buena Vista, Salida areas) 1920 Valley Drive, Pueblo, CO 81008 (719) 545-8737

South Platte Ranger District (Buffalo Creek Mountain Bike Area)
19316 Goddard Ranch Court, Morrison, CO 80465 (303) 697-0414

LOCAL CHAMBERS OF COMMERCE, TOURISM OFFICES

Local chambers of commerce and tourism agencies are good sources of recreation/travel/lodging information. Bicyclists wanting statewide bicycling information can call Bicycle Colorado, a non-profit organization formed to disseminate all kinds of information about Colorado biking.

STATEWIDE

Bicycle Colorado (General information on Colorado bicycling)
P.O. Box 3877, Littleton, CO 80131-3877 (303) 798-1429

Colorado Tourism Board
625 Broadway, Suite 1700, Denver, CO 80202 (303) 592-5410

Colorado Division of Parks and Outdoor Recreation (Colorado State Parks) 1313 Sherman St., Suite 618, Denver, CO 80203 (303) 866-3437

Colorado Hotel and Lodging Association (Lodging information, packages) 999 18th St., Denver, CO 80202 (303) 297-8335

Colorado Association of Cabins, Campgrounds & Lodges (Cabin, lodge rental information) 5101 Pennsylvania St., Boulder, CO 80303 (303)499-9343

LOCAL AGENCIES

Buena Vista, Upper Arkansas Valley

Buena Vista Chamber of Commerce
343 S. Highway 24, P.O. Box P, Buena Vista, CO 81211 (719) 395-6612

Heart of the Rockies Chamber of Commerce
406 W. Rainbow Blvd., Salida, CO 81202 (719) 539-2068

Buffalo Creek area, Park County (Also: Fairplay, Kenosha Pass areas)

Park County Regional Tourism Office
P.O. Box 701, Fairplay, CO 80440 (719) 836-2771, ext. 203

Denver/Boulder area

Denver Metro Convention & Visitors Bureau
225 W. Colfax Ave., Denver, CO 80202 (303) 892-1505

Boulder Chamber of Commerce
*40 Pearl Street, Boulder, CO 80302 (303) 442-1044

Georgetown

Georgetown Chamber of Commerce
P.O. Box 444, Georgetown, CO 80444

Leadville

Leadville/Lake County Chamber of Commerce
P.O. Box 861, 809 Harrison Ave., Leadville, CO 80461 (719) 486-3900

Pikes Pike, Colorado Springs areas

Pikes Peak Country Attractions Association
354 Manitou Ave., Manitou Springs, CO 80829 (719) 685-5854

Colorado Springs Chamber of Commerce
P.O. Drawer B, Colorado Springs, CO 80901 (719) 635-1551

Jefferson County (Evergreen, Golden, Morrison)

Jefferson County Open Space
700 Jefferson County Parkway, Suite 100, Golden, CO 80401 (303) 271-5925

West Chamber of Commerce
10140 W. Colfax, No.1, Lakewood, CO (303) 233-5555

Summit County (Breckenridge, Dillon)

Breckenridge Chamber of Commerce
555 S. Columbine, Box 1909, Breckenridge, CO 80424 (303) 453-6018

Lake Dillon Resort Association
121 Dillon Mall, Suite 102, P.O. Box 446, Dillon, CO 1-800-365-6365

Summit County Chamber of Commerce
P.O. Box 214, Frisco, CO 80443 (303) 468-6205

Winter Park/Grand County

Winter Park / Fraser Valley Chamber of Commerce
P.O. Box 3236, Winter Park, CO 80482 (303) 726-4118

Grand County Marketing and Economic Development Corporation
P.O. Box 227, Granby, CO 80446

NOTES

ORDER FORM FOR BIKE WITH A VIEW

Order additional copies of **BIKE WITH A VIEW** directly from the publisher, Concepts in Writing, for **$12.95** each.

Shipping:

$2.25 for the first book and 75 cents for each additional book — allow three to four weeks.

Or:

$4.25 for priority mail for **one** or **two** books; $4.25 ea. additional book — allow five to seven working days.

Taxes:

Colorado residents add 90 cents sales tax for each book.

Please send me _____ copies of **BIKE WITH A VIEW**.

Make your ☐ Check or ☐ Money Order out to Concepts in Writing.

_____ X $12.95= _____

_____ X .90= _____ Colorado resident tax per book

Shipping charges= _____

Total enclosed: _____

Name: _____

Address: _____

City: _____ State: _____ Zip: _____

Send check or money order to:

Concepts In Writing
1135 So. Garfield Street
Denver, CO 80210

(303)757-0269

ORDER FORM FOR **BIKE WITH A VIEW**

Order additional copies of **BIKE WITH A VIEW** directly from the publisher, Concepts in Writing, for **$12.95** each.

Shipping:

$2.25 for the first book and 75 cents for each additional book — allow three to four weeks.

Or:

$4.25 for priority mail for **one** or **two** books; $4.25 ea. additional book — allow five to seven working days.

Taxes:

Colorado residents add 90 cents sales tax for each book.

Please send me _____ copies of **BIKE WITH A VIEW**.

Make your ☐ Check or ☐ Money Order out to Concepts in Writing.

_____ X $12.95= _____

_____ X .90= _____ Colorado resident tax per book

Shipping charges= _____

Total enclosed: _____

Name: _____

Address: _____

City: _____ State: _____ Zip: _____

Send check or money order to:

Concepts In Writing
1135 So. Garfield Street
Denver, CO 80210

(303)757-0269